Please Don't Send Me to AFRICA

LEARNING TO FOLLOW GOD'S LEADING

Anna McGuckin

Copyright © 2016 Anna McGuckin.

Author photo courtesy of Bethany Coumos

All rights reserved. No part of this book may be used or reproduced by any means, graphic, electronic, or mechanical, including photocopying, recording, taping or by any information storage retrieval system without the written permission of the author except in the case of brief quotations embodied in critical articles and reviews.

Scriptures taken from the Holy Bible, New International Version®, NIV®. Copyright © 1973, 1978, 1984, 2011 by Biblica, Inc.™ Used by permission of Zondervan. All rights reserved worldwide. www.zondervan.com The "NIV" and "New International Version" are trademarks registered in the United States Patent and Trademark Office by Biblica, Inc.™ All rights reserved.

WestBow Press books may be ordered through booksellers or by contacting:

WestBow Press
A Division of Thomas Nelson & Zondervan
1663 Liberty Drive
Bloomington, IN 47403
www.westbowpress.com
1 (866) 928-1240

Because of the dynamic nature of the Internet, any web addresses or links contained in this book may have changed since publication and may no longer be valid. The views expressed in this work are solely those of the author and do not necessarily reflect the views of the publisher, and the publisher hereby disclaims any responsibility for them.

Any people depicted in stock imagery provided by Thinkstock are models, and such images are being used for illustrative purposes only. Certain stock imagery © Thinkstock.

ISBN: 978-1-5127-5945-7 (sc)
ISBN: 978-1-5127-5946-4 (e)

Library of Congress Control Number: 2016916597

Print information available on the last page.

WestBow Press rev. date: 10/12/2016

Contents

Dedication… vii
Acknowledgements… ix
Special Thank you… xi

Chapter 1   I Forgot… 1
Chapter 2   In the Beginning 4
Chapter 3   Our First Missions Trip 9
Chapter 4   My First Six Months in Mozambique 15
Chapter 5   The Six Months Continue 21
Chapter 6   Returning to Mozambique 29
Chapter 7   The Little Ones 37
Chapter 8   Lessons 44
Chapter 9   The Day of the Bombs 48
Chapter 10 Mothering 58
Chapter 11 Mice, Spiders and Snakes!! 71
Chapter 12 "I was sick and you looked after me…" ... 75
Chapter 13 Life in Mozambique 84
Chapter 14 The Closing of a Chapter 95

Dedication...

This book is dedicated to my loving parents, Greg and Polly, who did not think I was crazy when I said I felt God wanted me to be a missionary. My mom sent packages and letters and scrapbooks to me. My dad scouted out Mozambique with me, came to visit me, and encouraged me all along the way! I am so grateful to have been brought up in a loving home centered around God and being a family.

I would also like to dedicate this book to Steve and Ros Lazar, directors at the Iris Ministries Zimpeto base. They taught me to stay soft, even after years of serving God through struggles, tears and hardship. They taught me to laugh and find the joys and treasures God gives us in everyday life. I am so blessed to have learned from them and served with them during the three and a half years I spent in Mozambique.

Acknowledgements...

After returning from Mozambique in 2009 to live in Ohio, my dad encouraged me to write a book about my experiences in Africa. The thought was kind of daunting. I wasn't sure how to compile three and a half years of life in a book. There were so many stories I could have included, but did not. There are so many names I could have, perhaps should have mentioned, but did not. I prayed a lot through writing this book, asking God to inspire me with stories that should be written, and that would touch people's hearts. I did not name every single missionary or Mozambican I worked with, as I am sure I would leave someone out and feel terrible about it! But if I worked alongside you in Mozambique, you know who you are! I am so blessed to have you as family, to have gone through thick and thin with you, to have had late night popcorn parties in the kitchen, to have run out of the house screaming with you when a mouse ran across the floor, to have comforted each other during death and hardships, and to have prayed with you and experienced this incredible journey with you! Thank you for your friendship!

I would like to extend recognition to those of you who supported me prayerfully and financially the entire time I was in Mozambique. Your partnership produced fruit that will last for eternity, and I am so grateful for all you did for me. I often felt like I was going as a missionary for those who could not going themselves—an extension of those at home who were sending me.

My grandparents and relatives were all very interested in what I was doing overseas. My grandpa even learned Portuguese so we could communicate together! From family, to friends, to complete strangers who prayed for me, sent me checks, or left encouraging notes on my blog, I want to say thank you! This book is written for you, too!

Special Thank you...

...to my husband, Josiah. He kindly took a copy of my book to proof read and edit for me (before we started dating!). And he surprised me by typing up the whole book after our computer crashed and we lost the original document.

Thank you for pointing me to Christ every day, and for making me feel so loved and cared for. I can't wait to see the journey God takes us on together. I love you, m'dear fellow!

To check out my blog, and to read more of the journal entries you will find in this book visit: http://www.annacoumos.blogspot.com

Chapter 1

I Forgot...

I forgot that I am living in one of the poorest countries in the world. Not just a "third world country," Mozambique is on the list of the fifteen poorest countries (as of 2011).

Somehow, after living here for three years, it only just occurred to me yesterday that I really live in a developing nation, with the very poorest of people. Yes, I know they don't live like Americans. I know they live in little one or two room grass huts or cinder block houses. I know they are lucky to eat two meals a day, and there is a very large percentage of unemployment. I know the average monthly salary is about sixty dollars.

But yesterday, it all just really hit me. I was walking home from visiting an old man in the community who I help look after. I had just shared a Bible story at his house with five little kids who had followed me there. Every time I walk in the community I have a group of "followers." There are about thirty of these sweet little kids (thirty that know me) in the community behind our center, and when they see me, they come running, shouting, *"É o malungu Mana Anna!"* "It's the white Mana Anna!" On my walk home, I encountered several more of the children. Then I heard from behind a row of thorn bushes, "Mana Anna, come see what we are doing!" I came around to see. There were about eight or ten kids gathered around two very tiny cooking fires they had made with little twigs. And on these two miniature cooking fires they had cut a pop can in half, to use as a cooking pot and they were boiling the potato peelings from the potatoes their mothers were cooking on real fires for their dinner. They were pretending to be cooking dinner. These children were so excited to show me their play, and one of the mothers came over to greet me, and we both laughed at the fun these kids were having.

That's when it hit me. *Do these kids know they are the poorest of the poor? Do they know they are the ones on the bottom of the list? That they are considered hopeless?*

Compassion is not feeling sorry for someone; *it is having hope for them.* When I see these happy kids, running around in filthy clothes that fit them two years ago and certainly don't now — clothes that are full of holes. When I see these dirty little bare feet, I can't see them as poor. Because I see their sparkling eyes, and I have so much hope for them! The sweet little dirty hand that slips into mine and walks along beside me. The hungry hearts of kids who sit and feed off the story of Jesus calling the little children to come sit on his lap, because he loves them. The joy in their voices as they laugh and play, and say "Look! Here comes Mana Anna!" And when I must leave them, they say, "We will see you next time!"

Oh, the love I have for these kids. This country is called the poorest of the poor. But to God, they are the richest of the rich. They are the ones with the most hope. They are the ones Jesus was talking about when He said, "Blessed are the poor in spirit, for theirs is the kingdom of heaven" (Matthew 5:3).

CHAPTER 2

In the Beginning

I grew up in a family of ten children. I was number four, and the second daughter. Growing up, I had two passions: writing stories, and playing mommy. I loved to write, and my plan was to grow up, get married, have lots of children, live in a yellow farmhouse with a white wraparound porch, and author children's books. I held on to that dream from the time I was about six until I was thirteen. I had just finished school for the day (my mom home-schooled all of us!) and was putting my books away on my desk in the upstairs hall. I was daydreaming again of the children's books I would write, and about living with my many children in the yellow farmhouse. Then something occurred to me. *Maybe I should ask God if that is His plan for me?* So I did. I asked God what HE wanted me to do when I grow up.

Sometimes I feel God speak loud and clear to me. This was one of those times. I felt God say, "I want you to be a missionary and tell others about Me. I want you to be a mother to children who don't have a mother." I was shocked. We knew missionaries, and when they would come to visit, all I heard from their stories was "dinner plate-sized tarantulas… snakes hiding in the kitchen cupboards." "Are you SURE, God?" I asked. "Don't you want me to write children's books and have kids and live on a farm?" I went into my room, picked up my Bible, and asked God to please show me for sure that He wanted me to be a missionary. I let my Bible fall open and looked down to see the passage my eyes fell on. It was Matthew 28:18-20: "Then Jesus came to them and said, 'All authority in Heaven and on earth has been given to Me. Therefore, go and make disciples of all nations, baptizing them in the name of the Father, and of the Son, and of the Holy Spirit, and teaching them to obey everything I have commanded you. And surely I will be with you always, even to the end of the age.'"

"Okay, Lord," I said. "I will be a missionary, but I don't want to! You will have to give me a heart for that."

I went back to my normal chores, but my mind was spinning. For one thing, how could I tell anyone that I was supposed to be a missionary? I wasn't good enough to be a missionary! What would people think? I still argued with my siblings and would let my temper get the best of me. I was a sinner (the worst of them), and you had to be really good and Godly to be a missionary. I knew my faults better than anyone, and I knew I wasn't missionary material. And besides, I was terrified of little daddy long legs and had to call my brothers to squish them for me. How would I live in foreign countries where the spiders are all one hundred times larger than our spiders?! Of course, our missionary friends who told us those stories had been missionaries to Africa. "Well, Africa has enough missionaries," I decided. So I told God I would be a missionary, and I would go anywhere He wanted to send me — except Africa.

I didn't tell anyone about this shift in direction. I was too nervous that I would not measure up to what a missionary was. Then on Memorial Day, our 4-H club was driving a float in the parade. All of the 4-H'ers were supposed to dress up as what they wanted to be when they grew up, and they were asked to wear signs around their necks with the title. There were doctors and nurses, veterinarians, teachers and various other careers. I got ready to go and put my sign around my neck—"Author." I felt like I was lying. I knew in my heart that I was really going to be a missionary. I felt so much conviction about being a missionary that I made a new sign and came downstairs to leave. My mom noticed that I had written "Missionary" on this sign. She asked me if that was really what I wanted to be. I had to tell her. I was surprised that she did not give me the reaction I was expecting! As a matter of fact, nobody did! No one thought that it was silly or that I wasn't good enough to be a missionary. (Come to find out, you don't have to be "good enough" when the Lord calls you to something. He doesn't call the qualified people; instead He qualifies and equips those whom He calls!)

The Lord was faithful, and He began to change me and give me a heart for missions. I started reading every missionary biography or autobiography I could get my hands on. I started imagining opening orphanages like George Mueller did, living without running water and electricity, dreaming of the future. And I started yearning to get my feet wet. I just *had* to go on a short-term missions trip!

I began praying about where I was going to go, and I started searching for short-term missions opportunities.

In October of 2000, when I was fourteen years old, we had a guest speaker at our church. He was speaking on the Father heart of God, but what captured my attention was this little missionary lady he kept talking about. Her name was Heidi Baker. She had gone with her husband to Mozambique after the war ended. They had gone without much money and opened an orphanage. Now she and her husband had hundreds of orphanages in Mozambique and all over Africa, as well as many churches they had planted. Wow! That was just what I wanted to do—only not in Africa. At the closing of the conference, we found out that Heidi Baker was going to be speaking at a church near us the following month. I was so excited!

November came, and my sister Bonnie, some of her friends, and I drove to the church to hear Heidi speak. We watched a video on a little television about the orphanages she and her husband had opened. Then she spoke. And I knew that I wanted to do just what she and her husband were doing: taking care of children who had no families. Only I would not be going to Africa.

In December, I went to Acquire the Fire, a big youth conference. Our youth group went, and after one of the speakers shared, they were showing a video on the screen about YWAM (Youth With A Mission) short-term missions opportunities. The little children in the video they were showing on the screen were African children, and as I sat there moved by the video, I felt the Lord ask me, "Would you go to Africa if I asked you to?" "Yes, Lord!" I replied, "But you would have to give me the heart for Africa." In that very moment, He did just that. I was so glad that the lights were off because I didn't want anyone to see the tears streaming down my face.

As soon as I got home I began looking up this "Iris Ministries" that Rolland and Heidi Baker had started. I was certain I was going to go there. I read the stories on the website and learned how I could go on a short-term missions trip to one of the orphanages. I was making plans, but the Lord was to direct my steps.

My hope was that, by summer of 2002, I would be able to go to Mozambique. The Lord had different plans. In May of 2002, my mom came down with a strange paralysis called Guillain-Barre Syndrome. She lost the feeling of her nerves, was unable to walk, and was hospitalized for a week. She then moved to a rehab facility for two weeks. This was a very intense time for our family, but the Lord took such good care of us and brought so many of our relatives and loving friends around to care for us. After six months, my mom was fully recovered.

I was so set on going to Mozambique, Africa. I had shared this with my parents, and my dear dad was not at all on board with me. "Why don't you go somewhere closer, like South America?" he asked me. "But dad, God called me to Africa!" I protested. I was having trouble finding anyone to go with me on this missions trip, and as I was not yet eighteen years old, I had to be accompanied by an adult. Finally my dad told me, "If you can raise the money, I will go with you." To me, that meant we were going. To dad, he thought *There. That takes care of it. That will never happen.* But by Christmas, I had raised more than enough money for both of our airfares! We got our passports and sent our applications to the orphanage, and on March 6th, 2003, just before my seventeenth birthday, we were on our way!

CHAPTER 3

Our First Missions Trip

It was a snowy day when mom took us to the airport. I was so excited I could hardly stop smiling. We flew from Akron Canton to Atlanta, Georgia, and then took an eighteen-hour flight from Atlanta to Johannesburg, South Africa. It was a short flight from Johannesburg into Maputo, Mozambique. First thing was to collect our luggage. We waited in the very hot and stuffy little airport, as the luggage was unloaded. Pretty soon they were shutting the doors and the conveyor belt stopped. None of our four suitcases had arrived! We made our way out of the airport and were soon greeted by Laura, Christine and another missionary from Iris Ministries. It was so delightful to finally meet those I had been emailing with for months! We explained our situation with the luggage, and they took us to a desk where a large crowd of people were gathered, trying to get information about where their luggage was. We waited in what hardly resembled an organized line. People were cutting in and squeezing to the front, just a bit chaotic! Christine waited with us while the others went to gather a team of guys who had arrived on the same flight. While we were waiting, Christine got a phone call that her house had been broken into. She left in one of the vehicles and contacted the others to let them know that we would be returning with them. Dad discovered if we slipped around the desk and crowd of people, there was a little room with a man at a desk. Maybe he could help us? In we went and tried to explain our situation. Unfortunately, this man did not speak much English. He reached under his desk and pulled out a laminated page full of pictures of various types of luggage. "Like this?" he asked, pointing to a picture of luggage. "No, no," we answered, "it's bigger!" "Like this?" he asked, pointing to the next picture. Finally he retrieved a piece of paper and had us fill it out, and we understood that we should come back in two days to see if our luggage had arrived.

That taken care of, we went back out to find the missionaries who were waiting for us. We walked through the small airport twice, and then checked outside. They were not there! Apparently, they had come to check for us in line, but as we were not there, they assumed we had left with Christine. They had taken our carry-on backpacks, so all we had were the fanny packs we were wearing. We waited outside on the curb in the heat, hoping they would realize we were not there and come back for us. Taxi drivers kept asking us if we needed a ride, but we didn't even know where we were going! After a couple hours, it was getting dark. We knew we had to figure something out. I dug through my fanny pack and finally found an old piece of paper from the Iris website with a phone number on it. We found a phone room and made the call, but the man who answered was not from Iris Ministries. We were walking out of the phone room, not sure what to do, when the man at the desk called us back in. In his broken English, he explained that the guy we had called just called him back and had the phone number for Iris Ministries. The man let us make a call free of charge, and finally someone was on the way to get us.

Soon we were driving dangerously down bumpy roads, narrowly missing pedestrians who didn't seem to notice the cars speeding by. We made it to Shop Rite, the local grocery store. We were ushered through the store while our new missionary friend pretty much filled our cart for us (mostly packages of ramen noodles!), and 15 minutes later, we were back in the car and heading to the orphanage. As we drove, we asked lots of questions. "What will we do at the orphanage?" I asked. "You will know what to do," our driver answered.

The sun sets pretty early in Mozambique, so it was completely dark outside when we arrived around 8:00 that evening. Pulling into the center, we drove around the caniso reed school buildings and the church. Our missionary friend drove us up to the door of the short-term compound. As soon as we opened the doors of the truck, we were surrounded by lots of children. "What is your name? My name is... How long are you here for?" So many children to greet us! After being shown to our rooms and given a small tour of the short-term compound, we soon collapsed into our beds feeling relieved and overwhelmed at the same time. (Our luggage did arrive two days later)

Those two weeks we spent in Mozambique were so special and amazing! We got to know so many kids at the center, learned stories, met many wonderful long-term and short-term missionaries, and made so many new friends! We went to the local garbage dump to minister to the people who lived there. I remember how hot it was, and flies were everywhere.

After gathering people from up on top of the dump, we went down to Iris Ministries' little caniso reed church at the outskirts of the dump. After a short service where Heidi Baker gave a message, we passed out bread. All chaos broke out, and people were fighting over the bread and shoving each other to get a loaf. Then a few people started saying, "Quero água!" ("I want water!") Their voices were parched, and I had no idea when they had last had anything to drink. One of the missionaries took a jug of water and poured sips of it into their mouths. It broke my heart to see these thirsty people begging for a drink of water.

The real culture shock hit when we went out to do prison and street ministry. My dad and I both got to speak at the prison, and we prayed for the young fellows and passed out bread. Then we gathered outside a capalana shop (selling material for wrap skirt "capalanas") called Casa Elefante for street ministry. Soon a crowd of children and teenagers joined us. We sang a few songs, and as they sang in Portuguese and Shangaan (two languages I did not understand at all), I stood there looking at the faces of each of these young people. They lived on the streets. Some were barefoot or had mismatched flip-flops. Their clothes were torn and dirty, and their bodies were dirty. Many of them were probably just there for the free bread at the end (and if it were me, I am sure I would be there for the same reason!). One girl really captured my attention. She looked to be about fourteen years old—just a couple years younger than myself. She had a little baby she was feeding cookies to, and when the baby began to fuss, she nursed her right there in front of everyone (that is very normal to do in Africa). For me, it was so overwhelming to see this young little mommy living on the streets. What a hopeless life she had with most likely no one to guide her. She was just a kid, and she already had a child to raise!

That night I remember piling back into the pickup truck, driving through the dark and crowded streets, and falling into bed feeling like my head was spinning and my heart was overwhelmed.

Throughout the days, I got to play with the kids, hold babies in the baby house (though I only went there once because it was smelly and difficult for me to handle with all of those toddlers trying to climb on me), and I helped paint the boys' dorm rooms. My dad spent a lot of time working with two youth digging a trench to lay phone lines and installing telephone lines into the back row of missionary housing.

We got to spend an afternoon at the Indian Ocean one day, and my dad put one foot in the water and was stung by a jellyfish!

During this entire trip, I was so sure the Lord was calling me back to volunteer at this children's center. I got to spend a lot of time talking with Laura and Christine about what it was like to live there. I had another year before graduating high school, and I was definitely going to apply to come back after that.

The day we were leaving, my dad began vomiting and became very sick. Debbie, a missionary nurse, did a malaria quick test on him and announced, "Congratulations! You have malaria." She gave us medicine, and we left for the airport. On the way, we had to pull over so dad could throw up. He was so sick! We made it from Maputo to South Africa. At that point, dad was too sick to continue. He lay down on some chairs, and I went to an information desk to find some help. I explained the situation and went back to dad with their response. A man followed me who had also been waiting at the information desk. He reached dad and said, "I am a doctor. What's the problem?" God had surely arranged for him to be there at just the right moment! He told us there was a hospital just outside the airport, and that we could get someone with a wheelchair to take dad there. Soon a guy came and wheeled dad to the hospital. We were taken back to a little room where dad could lie down on a bed and sleep. We waited awhile, but there didn't seem to be any other patients being waited on. Finally I went to the desk and explained that our flight would be leaving soon, and we needed to be seen so we wouldn't miss our flight. Next thing, they gave dad a shot and some more medicine, and the guy came and wheeled dad back to the airport. We ran the whole way, and our flight happened to be delayed twenty minutes so we made it just in time!

Dad slept most of the trip home. It took about three weeks before he was totally back to his healthy self.

This was our first introduction to missions, and I was utterly changed inside from this experience. The Lord had shown me so much, and I had grown tremendous passion in my heart for missions and for future things He had called me to.

Chapter 4

My First Six Months in Mozambique

After this first missions trip, I was sure I would return to the same children's center as soon as I could. I finished up high school and graduated in June of 2004. Two weeks later, my dad and I were on our way back to Mozambique! I had applied to stay at the center for six months but was told I could only come for three months because I was so young. I was slightly disappointed, but I knew God wanted me to go—so for six months or three, I was thrilled to be returning!

On my application, one of the questions asked what I was interested in doing as a volunteer missionary at the center. I prayed a lot about this and really felt the Lord leading me to help out in the baby house. This was a huge step for me, because as a short-term visitor I had such a hard time being in the baby house. Don't get me wrong—I LOVE babies!! But the baby house seemed uncontrolled and chaotic. I had no idea what I could do to help.

We arrived and were greeted by many dear friends, all of whom somehow remembered us from among the roughly one thousand visitors a year who pass through the children's center! That first night as we were getting settled into our room, a teenage boy came looking for Papa Greg. He was so excited and greeted dad with a big bear hug. It was one of the boys—Pasqual—who had helped my dad dig trenches for phone lines the year before. He had grown so much in the last fifteen months that my dad barely recognized him!

I was introduced to Karen, who was now overseeing the baby house. I was pleased to find out that much had changed, and the baby house was cleaner and less chaotic now. But the toddlers still mobbed me—and everybody else coming to visit them—when I walked in the door. I was going to be helping in a few areas. I would mainly be working in the evenings during the bedtime routine. I remember the first afternoon Karen took me through the baby house. The babies were napping in their cribs, and she took me through each of the four bedrooms, telling me each of the little ones' names. I wondered if I would ever remember who was who!

I would also be helping Laura in the preschool. She taught the four-year olds from the baby house a few days a week. We would take the kids from the baby house to the common room in the big long-term house to have preschool. The kids found it great fun to steal Mana Laura's shoes, and then repeat her scolding them by chanting in English, "Give me my shoe! Give me my shoe!" It was hilarious to hear, but they were pretty accomplished at being naughty. They seemed to feed off each other, with a few instigators to get them going.

Helping Laura was fun, but my Portuguese was zero, so it was hard to enforce discipline.

After two weeks, the time came for my dear dad to head back home. He had come to help me get settled in, and for that I was so grateful! He was leaving on a better note than last year – no malaria this time! Before he left, we talked in my room while he packed. He told me if I was invited to stay for six months like I originally hoped, that would be fine. He also said I should not think of Ohio as my home. "Wherever you are is your home. It is not just in Ohio. It is here, or wherever God takes you." That was really profound, and it has helped me a lot ever since. At first, I was kind of bothered to hear that. After all, isn't home where my family is? But if that is how I look at it, I will always feel like I am away from home unless I am in Ohio with my family. Thankfully, while I love my family dearly and miss them so much when I am away from them, I am able to set up "home" wherever I am. And hopefully the peace of Christ and His love will help others to feel at home in my home.

The morning my dad left, my friend Christine arrived for a visit at the center (she is the one whose house was broken into while we waited in line for our missing baggage on the first trip). It was so nice to see a familiar face! We had written to each other since my first trip, and now she was there to help me see my dad off. I cried at the airport and watched until I couldn't see him anymore. That night, I slept in the girls' dorm, since I wasn't quite ready to sleep in my new room alone.

It wasn't hard to find a lot to do to fill up my time. I got well acquainted with each of the babies and toddlers in the baby house. I did learn all of their names, as well as each of their personalities. Then Laura was asked to become a dorm mom to the dorm of five to nine year old boys, and she asked me if I was comfortable to teach preschool on my own? At first, that was a little daunting. I didn't speak any Portuguese, and these darling kiddos could get quite out of hand! I took on the new role and it proved to be a lot of work, but I loved it.

Karen—who was a teacher herself—gave me lots of ideas and books and help. I learned what preschoolers should be learning before moving on to kindergarten, and began preparing lessons each evening and then studying my little Portuguese/English dictionary and writing down all the important words I would need. This was a great way to learn a language —by immersion. I also had a few simple Portuguese lessons from one of the missionaries. She did a great job explaining words and phrases to me and giving me some conversations I might have around the center.

A new room became available for me to teach the kids in. We turned the room down by the gate of the center into our preschool classroom. All of the tables, chairs and supplies were moved down there. Three mornings a week I would lead the ten four-year olds from the baby house down to the preschool room. It was quite a walk for their little legs. We would sing songs the whole way, and on really hot days I would bring water, and we would take a break halfway to have drinks. The walk was a good thing, however, as it wore them out enough that they were ready to sit still and listen during class. We worked on fine and gross motor skills, did crafts and learned shapes, colors, numbers, the alphabet, and how to write their names.

One morning we had just had tin can stilt races and made night and day posters, and were now sitting down on the esteira (caniso reed mat) for story time. The story was about a cat and a mouse. The cat was chasing the mouse, and then the cat opened his mouth and closed it right over the mouse. Suddenly one of the little girls burst into tears. I quickly turned the page to show them that the cat spits the mouse back out because they were just playing.

Timothy was the first to learn to write his name. I was so proud of him! He was very smart, so sometimes he would finish his work before the rest and would proceed to come up with ways to get the other kids in trouble. I began calling upon him as my helper to keep him from being naughty.

Helena, like Timothy, could be a handful as well. The two of them tended to get the rest of the children wound up very quickly.

Ivan was always looking for affirmation and loved to know when I was proud of him for his accomplishments. He longed for attention, and if not given enough healthy attention, he would turn to getting into trouble to be noticed. It was a lot of work to give him and all of the other children all the love and affirmation they needed, but it paid off because they became much better behaved.

One day after I had been there for about two months, another room opened up at the center in the short-term compound. At the missionary business meeting, the discussion came up on what to use the room for. I threw in my vote to use it for a preschool, and that seemed the best option. I was so thrilled! A few short-term missionaries who were visiting helped me scrub the room down and paint and decorate it. I couldn't wait to have our classes in the new room. It was perfect, with a blue countertop, a sink, and a tiny room in the back with shelves for storage. Besides that, the sidewalk and area outside the new classroom would be great for outdoor activities for the kids, such as sidewalk chalk or energetic games. A sweet short-term missionary I got to know offered to make curtains and mail them to me. She picked out adorable dark blue fabric with stars on it that matched the countertops and really made the room look finished.

CHAPTER 5

The Six Months Continue

I was so pleased with how everything was running with the preschool. The babies were growing, and I loved being at the center. But my three months were quickly coming to a close, and I was still feeling like I was supposed to be there for six months. After a lot of prayer, and encouragement from friends, I asked the directors of the center if I could meet to chat with them. We scheduled a time to meet—the evening before I was to leave for South Africa for my monthly visa stamp in my passport. Right before heading to their home, I received back a positive test result showing I had malaria (my second round). On top of being very nervous about asking them if I could stay longer, I felt sick from the malaria. Ros offered me chocolate cake, but I was so nervous that I forgot to eat it, and she ended up wrapping it for me to take with me. I had a nice long chat with Steve and Ros, and expressed to them my desire to stay on longer. They asked a lot of questions and in the end asked me to write them a letter; not stating what I would do for the next three months, but why I felt God wanted me to stay. I went back to my room and was up until two in the morning writing the letter. I cried and prayed, and wanted it to be just the right wording. I cant remember exactly what I wrote, but as I prayed, it basically boiled down to the fact that I didn't think God was done with whatever He was doing in and through me in Mozambique. I felt He wanted me to stay longer because He still had more for me there.

I left for South Africa with a missionary friend at 6 a.m. the following morning, and I gave the letter to someone to pass on to Steve and Ros. I was feeling pretty doubtful that I would be allowed to stay on because I was still so young, but I knew that whatever the Lord wanted for me would be.

At the bus station a couple of days later, Karen picked us up. We stopped at Shop Rite on the way back to the center, and Karen told me she had talked with Steve and Ros and that they had an answer for me. She asked if I wanted to know right away or wait. I told her I wanted to know right away, and she shared with me that they had decided I could stay on for three more months. I was elated!

I was given a few more responsibilities, including working in the donations room sorting and organizing the continuous flow of donated clothes, shoes, and various other items that we were so blessed to receive for our kids. I also began taking the three-year olds from the baby house for preschool on the two days I did not have the older kids.

The six months were flying by! I would be leaving in the middle of January, right before my older sister was due to have her first baby.

My update later in December 2004:

Merry Christmas from Anna!!

My dear family and friends,
I pray you all have a wonderful Christmas! Snow on the ground... Christmas trees up... Last-minute runs to the store, and standing in 20-minute checkout lines... Fresh baked Christmas cookies... Christmas pageants... Sounds of snow crunching beneath boots... Christmas presents... Long drives through the cold to visit family... Staring out the car windows at all the lit up houses covered in Christmas lights and decorations. New sweaters... Sucking on red and white-striped peppermint candy canes, trying to make the end pointy... Christmas songs playing softly in the background... A manger set on top of the mantle surrounded by swags of spruce and holly berries... Christmas.

Hard to imagine all of those wonderful things as I sit here in the house with the fan blowing directly on me, sucking ice cubes to stay cool. The thermometer says it's 100 degrees, and I believe it! I walked past George today, and he said, "It hasn't snowed yet." "But they're calling for it tonight!" I assured him, "a 70 percent chance. So we should still get our white Christmas!" Ha ha!

Christmas is going to be an exciting and amazing event here, and I am so excited! Tonight we have the candlelight service at church. The kids are all going up in groups to sing a Christmas song or do a skit. I've been working with the four-year olds in the baby house to do a special Christmas song. They are so precious and are really doing a fantastic job! I hope they don't get stage fright. After the service, the church will be set up with tables and decorated with streamers and balloons and maybe a Christmas tree, though we haven't bought it yet.

Tomorrow morning, the gift giving starts around 10:00. I will be assisting in the baby house and might move over to the girls' dorm when the babies are done. At 1:00, the kids from the bocaria (the city dump) arrive and get a chicken lunch in the church, followed by gifts prepared for them, and then we haul them back to the dump in the big flatbed truck.

Next our kids file into the church. They will sit at long tables, each get a big plate of chicken and rice and french fries, and a bottle of Coca-cola or Fanta. After everyone's tummies are quite full, they will have the afternoon to spend playing with their new gifts. The missionaries are getting together to watch "It's a Wonderful Life" and eat popcorn and Christmas cookies.

Sunday morning's church service will be a special one, as we are integrating about 60 kids back into their homes and families this year, and we are having a special service for them. Sunday evening the long-term missionaries are getting together to have a cookout, sing Christmas carols (like "I'm dreaming of a white Christmas" ;-)), and have a gift exchange.

Everyone is talking about it being Jesus's birthday. The preschoolers run up to me just to ask, "Is it Jesus's birthday yet?" then run off and play again.

Things are certainly different here for Christmas. I can imagine what's going on at home. Right now it's about 6:15 a.m., and mom is getting up to start getting the gifts and food packed to take to the grandparents' houses for our usual Christmas Eve get-togethers.

Tomorrow morning my brothers and sisters will be tiptoeing down the steps at 4:00 a.m. to sit on the couch with all the lights off except the Christmas tree lights. They will sit there talking quietly and staring at the beautifully lit Christmas tree, in great anticipation of mom and dad finally rolling out of bed to get the day started. Hopefully Cara or Christina will remember to put the coffee on so it doesn't take dad an extra 20 minutes.

Mom and dad will come in and turn on the light and put on the radio (WCRF's seven days of non-stop Christmas music, you know!). Dad will sit down with his Bible and read aloud the story of Jesus's birth from Luke. Then starting with Sammy (the youngest) and working their way up, each of my siblings will pass out the gifts they bought or made for each other. It is so special at our house. Everyone opens their gifts one at a time, and lots of "Oooh's" and "Ah's" are raised over each other's presents.

When the siblings are done, we clean up all the wrapping paper, then comes mom and dad's gifts. We again open the gifts one at a time, waiting for each person, and getting excited with them. When the Christmas presents are over, we clean up, everyone makes a place under the tree for their pile of gifts, and we spend the day playing with the new toys and games, wearing our new clothes, and being together as a family.

Mom makes a big lunch to have around 2:00, and Grandma Dorn comes over. Last year Grandma came on Christmas Eve and spent the night, so she was there for our special Christmas morning routine. That was so special.

God has blessed me with eighteen amazing Christmases at home with my absolutely AMAZING family. I can't believe I won't be there this year, but I am thrilled to be here. AND, my mom and dad consented to leaving the Christmas tree up until I get back, so that makes everything okay...☺

Well, right now I am going to the baby house. The kids just went down for their naps, and I am getting together with the tias, and decorating the whole baby house! I have garlands and streamers and balloons and Christmas lights, and a Christmas tree poster the kids made with their handprints. It'll be so beautiful when the kids wake up.

May the Lord bless you richly this Christmas. May His light shine ever brighter on you, and may you sing and make music in your heart to God! Don't be frustrated over burnt cookies or the wrong size clothes for someone. Just relax and enjoy your day. Sit and just ponder over our Savior's birth. Think about what it means to YOU personally. Thank God for His incredible gift to you. And think about what you can give back to Him for Christmas this year.

I love you all so much! Merry Christmas, Feliz Natal!
In Jesus, Love always,
Anna

* * *

At the end of December, a new baby arrived at the center. She was severely malnourished, and so skinny. They named her Anna. I used to sit at the computer with her in my arms while I worked on the hospitality emails. When she would cry it was such a faint and weak whimper. One night the missionary doctor came to me and said, "Your friend is sick." I followed the doctor to her room where little Anna was struggling to breathe. I sat down on the bed beside her and prayed for her. I knew that would be the last time I saw her. The next morning, just the day before I was leaving to go home, I found out she had passed away in the night. That was hard. Her little life had been cut short, but I knew she was now totally healed and with Jesus! I had always noticed how long her fingers were, and thought *She will be a piano player!* Maybe she is playing instruments of praise in Heaven?

It was Sunday. After church, a few of us missionaries went out to eat for lunch. I had a yummy salad with fresh mango slices on top. By the time we arrived back at the center, I wasn't feeling too well. I went up to the baby house to do the bedtime routine for one last time. I was feeling worse and worse and finally had to go back to my room where I began vomiting and having cold sweats. I was so nauseated. A nurse came and did a malaria test, which came back positive. My parents called to see how I was doing on my final night, but I was concentrating so hard on not throwing up that I could barely talk. That whole evening is a blur, except that some of the missionaries came to pray for me, and one of the missionary nurses took care of me. The next morning I felt great. It was such an answer to prayer! I was able to enjoy the Monday morning prayer meeting and say goodbyes to everyone.

After six amazing months in Mozambique, spending time doing crafts and painting nails and passing out snacks for the girls, caring for babies, teaching preschool, and so much more, it was time for me to leave. I was sure I would be back sometime, to volunteer longer term. I was going to miss my dear kids, my

Mozambican friends, and my missionary friends so much! But I was also certain I would be back, and that made the going a little easier. And I had my first new niece due to be born in a few weeks to look forward to.

Chapter 6
Returning to Mozambique

After returning to my family in Ohio, I began looking for a job. This would be my first "real" job since graduating high school. I had grown to enjoy teaching the preschoolers in Mozambique, so I felt it would be logical to look for a job perhaps as a preschool teacher's assistant. One day my friend's mom called me. She knew I had returned from Africa and was probably looking for a job. She wanted to let me know that there was a position available at a Christian school for a teacher's assistant in the preschool. I could not believe it—this would be perfect! And here I was being offered the position! I told her I would call her back soon.

Now, sometimes what seems perfect from our viewpoint is not what God has in store. For some reason, even though the job seemed exactly right for me, I did not have peace about accepting the position. I just couldn't figure out why. After praying, I really felt I was not to take the job, even though I did not understand what God was doing when this seemed so good. I called my friend's mom back, thanked her for thinking of me, but told her I just didn't have peace from God for this job. She was kind and understanding. The following Sunday, a dentist friend from church approached me. He said he had been praying and felt God wanted him to train me to be a dental assistant. Would I be interested? I could hardly believe it! I knew right away that this was the reason God did not want me to take the other job. It was not that there was anything wrong with the teaching position. But God had something else he wanted for me to do. I had to be obedient in turning down the first job, and trust God for the right job—and now I was seeing the answer. Sometimes it is so hard to be obedient and trust when we cannot see what God is doing. But God will never let you down if you are obediently following Him.

Over the next year, I was trained on the job at the dentist office. I learned so many valuable skills during that time! The dentist was very good at teaching, so while we were waiting for patients who were late, or if there were cancellations and we had free time, he would be drawing on the white board and explaining in detail about teeth, root canals, cavities and extractions. I learned the instruments used for each procedure, how to set up and clean up rooms, and how to take and develop dental X-rays. I learned how to sterilize the instruments. The receptionist/dental assistant who also worked there taught me a lot about insurance companies, filing systems and receiving payments. We were a good team, and I really enjoyed the dental work. I got to know many of the patients very well. We had lots of opportunities to pray for people at the office, and not just care for their teeth. Sometimes a patient would sit down in the exam chair and start pouring out to us their life's story. Before you knew it, tears were streaming down their face, and we would listen and pray and offer any wisdom for the situation.

I enjoyed the dental office work and being with my family and friends, but I still felt God calling me back to Africa. I applied to go back indefinitely as a "long-term" missionary. A couple days before Christmas in December of 2005, I received a telephone call to let me know that my application had been accepted, and I could start making plans to return to Mozambique. Words cannot express the elation I felt!

In May of 2006, I left my job at the dental office, as well as my family, friends and church, and headed back to my beloved Mozambican family.

I was so warmly welcomed back at the center. Some of the missionaries had prepared a room for me, and left flowers on my table. I was so happy to see so many familiar faces, and how the babies were growing so fast.

I started out helping in the baby house again, and assisting another missionary in preparing preschool lesson plans. One of the Mozambican ladies had taken over the teaching when I left in 2005. She was doing a wonderful job with the children.

A dental team was about to arrive for two weeks of dental clinics, and as I had just been working as a dental assistant, I was asked to help the team out. There were two dentists on the team, as well as a few others who came to volunteer however they could. We made plans to spend a week at our center doing checkups on our kids, as well as on the kids from the community who attended our school. The second week would be spent on dental outreaches to another children's center, and to a village nearby. The first week went pretty smoothly. We set up exam rooms in the clinic on our base and did several extractions, root canals and fillings. The team had brought a small generator-powered contraption complete with a drill and suction! They were well equipped for the primitive accommodations we had.

The following week, we took our equipment and headed to Machava, a smaller Iris children's center. The first day, the generator provided for us there was not working, so we had to limit our services to just exams and extractions. The second day we had a working generator, so we were able to provide more care for the children and adults who came. The last day of our outreaches, we set up in a small, empty one-room reed school. We had two tables we used for the patients to lie on while we worked on their teeth. It was quite primitive, and we had a pressure cooker to sterilize instruments (and lots of bleach!). Some of the patients we saw had never been to a dentist before, so the most difficult part was helping them to relax and sometimes holding and calming a crying child who was afraid to open his mouth. We gave out balloons and stickers to the kids. We saw about 70 patients each day, and by the end of the two weeks, we were all quite exhausted. But it was so thrilling to put these fresh skills I had been learning for the last year into practical use on the mission field!

At the end of our dental outreaches, Ros came to speak to me about an idea she had been praying about. The girls' dorm had a small apartment attached to it for the missionary looking after the girls to live in. Debbie was a nurse who lived there for a few years and put a lot of good things in place in the girls' area. Then she went back to the United States, and another missionary moved in temporarily to care for the girls. She was also a nurse. But it was becoming obvious that to handle all of the medical needs as well as all of the everyday housekeeping needs for the girls was too much for one person. They wanted to put someone in the girls' dorm who was not a nurse. Ros was asking if I would pray about doing that.

I knew right away that this was what God had called me back to Mozambique for. I moved into the girls' dorm apartment a few days later. The Lord gave me a neat dream that first night in my new "home." In the dream, Debbie was building a rectangular box out of bricks for a flower garden. She was putting each brick into place, and Liz was helping her. The next scene in my dream was the missionary nurse I was replacing in the girls' dorm. She was pouring dirt into the box for the garden to grow in. Then I came along and started planting flowers in the new garden. It was such a sweet dream, and the Lord showed me that Debbie and Liz had been instrumental in laying a foundation in the girls' dorm and putting boundaries in place. The next missionary fulfilled her role by putting onto the foundation a place for the girls to grow. Now I was getting to come along and do my part (planting things). Someday, someone else would come and build on what I did. Each of our roles was so important. The others who had gone before me had done well what they were called to do. I felt like I had the easy job. But all of it was necessary for the girls at our center to grow and thrive!

I was so excited to begin these new responsibilities. I started getting to know the girls better, trying hard to learn each of their names. For a while I thought *If I forget a girl's name, I will just call her Maria or Marta.* There were so many Maria's and Marta's in the girls' dorm at that time that I had a pretty good chance of getting it right with one of those names ;-).

I was not the only missionary working with the girls. A missionary nurse and the rest of the medical staff still handled a lot of their medical issues. Nancy helped with monthly birthday parties, and gave the girls milk and healthy treats on a regular basis. Alex and Ellie—a wonderful missionary couple—became dear friends to me, and Ellie and I worked together with the girls. We did clothing swap one day a week —swapping out worn and tattered clothes with nicer donated clothes, or giving out clothes to girls who didn't have much. We also began a discipleship program for the girls. We had three groups: the little girls, the middle girls and the oldest girls. We would meet with the discipleship groups each week and have Bible lessons together. Getting the girls into smaller groups, asking age-appropriate questions, getting to know their individual personalities in smaller group settings: these times were so special. Ellie and I treasured these opportunities to teach and raise the girls up to begin a relationship with God and to get to know Him better.

A Very Special Day!
(Blog journal entry – July 22, 2006)

Today Nancy and I had a party to celebrate three birthdays for three very special little girls! They each received invitations for their party, and have been asking me about it all week. I've been looking forward to it as much as they have! One of the girls just arrived last week. She has never had a birthday party before. She was grinning from ear to ear the whole time!

The girls were given princess treatment today. Each girl got to choose fancy clothes to wear (from my bag of special occasion clothes). They opened their gifts to find hair bands, chap stick, candy, stick-on earrings, and beads with string. Just what little girls love! We had spaghetti and salad for lunch on glass dishes with forks, and pop poured in glass cups. (Here they eat with plastic plates and use their hands or spoons.)

We made pretty crepe paper flowers, played "Pass the parcel" with a present wrapped in layers, and in each layer they got either candy or a task (like jumping on one foot or singing a song). After unwrapping the last layer, they found a colorful new jump rope, which they were thrilled to play with. We played other games, and they ran around the big yard chasing balloons and laughing. Afterwards they sat quietly drawing pictures and writing on paper, while eating cookies and absorbing the attention of missionaries and a sweet Mozambican dorm parent.

It was so fun separating them from the 400 children living here, making them the center of attention and celebrating their lives. It is amazing to show these girls God's love for them! Every day is such a joy. I love it!

* * *

Throughout the three years I worked in the girls' dorm, many others were involved in the care and teaching of the girls. A sweet missionary came for a while and did sewing and gardening with the girls, and she was also instrumental in the purchase of a stove for them. With the stove, we were able to have the tias teach the girls each Saturday to cook and prepare meals.

Betty and her husband Bob came to teach sewing for the girls and carpentry for the boys. Betty did a remarkable job teaching several of the girls on a weekly basis how to sew very well.

A dear elderly Mozambican lady came when she could to teach crocheting and embroidery. She had a heart to work with the girls and would regularly come to visit me and get supplies for the girls she was teaching.

A missionary friend from another ministry would sometimes come with some of her Mozambican friends to teach at our discipleship meetings.

Many others played various roles in the lives of these girls, all pouring into them life skills and valuable lessons to build strong, rich roots to help them grow in Christ and set them on the path God has for each of them.

CHAPTER 7

The Little Ones

Part 1 – Sina

One day Tracey, who was in charge of the baby house, was in the city. I got a phone call that a new baby was arriving in the baby house—since Tracey was away, would I please go there to receive the new baby? We had already heard that this little one was coming, but we were not quite prepared for how little she would be. I headed up to the baby house, and the person who brought her placed the tiny baby, wrapped up in several layers of capalana, into my arms. Sina was five weeks old when she arrived. She was very light, even when wrapped up in the big capalana. As we lay her on the changing table and began unwrapping her, we found she was literally just skin and bones. Her little baby face, which should have been chubby and healthy, was tight and old looking. Her little legs were bones covered in skin. She was so small and frail! The nurses examined her and made a feeding schedule to start plumping her up and getting her healthy. We also made a plan for the "Mommies" to do night shifts. The Mommies were those of us missionaries who were able to do night shifts with malnourished babies that arrived. Whenever a new little one arrived who required extra care and attention, we would start a schedule for night shifts and day shifts. I loved doing that, even though it meant some sleepless nights now and then.

We did Sina's feedings every three hours during the day, and every four hours throughout the night. We had a little "Moses Basket" for her to sleep in, on a little cushion. She was so tiny in that basket. When our shift was over, we would make sure there were diapers and clean clothes in her basket, and pass her on to the next "Mommy" who got to care for her.

With her nutrition improving, Sina put on weight quickly and became the joy and delight of all of us who were privileged to be her "mommies." She was a little bundle of sweetness. Her eyes sparkled, she smiled, she cooed, and she attached herself to the hearts of everyone who got to spend time with her. It was kind of sad when she was strong enough to not need the overnight shifts anymore, but also exciting that she could move into the baby house with the healthy children.

Sina grew and had lots of excited mamas rejoicing over each milestone. She learned to sit up, then to crawl, and eventually she was walking and running in the baby house with the rest of the toddlers. She had quite the personality bubbling out!

Her mother was HIV+ and died in childbirth. When Sina was tested for HIV, she was found to be negative – just another miracle God had worked in Sina's life!

Watching miracles unfold in her life has grown my faith in God as I see how He heals and brings life!

Sina is one story. There are many more. We had the privilege of caring for so many little ones. Some we loved back to health, and some we loved for a short time on this earth, giving them the best last days here before they were carried into the arms of Jesus. Each child is a gift from God. To care for their basic needs of being fed, diaper changes, baths, and cuddles, was truly a gift to me. What a privilege to be a mother to babies whose earthly mama was unable to be there for them—whether she died or was ill, or for other reasons—and to fill a role that is very necessary in a baby's life. I am so blessed to have had those opportunities!

Part 2 – God brings more children

One day, I went with Ros to check out a children's center we had heard about. The children there were very neglected. Some were wearing soiled diapers that had obviously not been changed in quite awhile. They smelled and lay on mats on the sand, and flies were buzzing everywhere. Some of the kids had no clothes on. Many of them had mental and physical challenges. After this first visit, Ros would head to the children's center on a weekly basis, bringing little gifts of candy or stuffed animals, trying to be friendly and to build a relationship with them. One day, Ros spoke with the man in charge and asked if we could take some of the sickliest children to our center to help them grow stronger and healthier, explaining that we have a clinic and trained nurses who could give these children the care they required. The first little one we received from that center was Zephaniah. He was three years old. They told us he was paralyzed on his left side and couldn't walk. He was such a sad little fellow. He sat up and would say over and over in a weak voice, "Quero água. Quero água." ("I want water. I want water.") I remember holding him, and he weakly rested his little head on my chest, and my heart melted for him. A few different missionaries worked with him very diligently, and in just three-and-a-half weeks, his scabies were cleared up, and he put on eight pounds and began walking on his own! One day, I walked into the baby house, and he stood up and very slowly and wobbly walked to me to ask for water! I wanted to cry with joy. His constant blank expression and cranky personality was transformed into a joyful little boy. He would laugh all the time and loved to hold hands and give hugs.

The next little boy to come was suffering very badly from various illnesses. He immediately started tests at the hospital and treatment for his conditions. He was soon walking like Zephaniah. His personality shone as he got healthier. His name means "happy little one" – which was certainly true with his smiles and laughter.

The third miracle child from that center came on October 16, 2006. Ros asked the director for a little boy named Zachariah who was about five or six years old. He lay on a reed mat all day, rolling his head back and forth (perhaps to keep the flies off his face, which were constantly buzzing around him and landing on his lips). Consequently, he had a scar on the back of his head from being left on the mat. Ros asked if we could just bring him for a few hours to our center so he could have a physical exam by the Mozambican doctor at our clinic. He consented to this, and she brought him to the center. I looked after him all that afternoon, fed him, bathed him, and prayed for him. The doctor said he had a very bad ear infection in both ears (which was causing him to smell). He had pneumonia and horrible scabies. We took him back to the other center late in the afternoon and explained that, in his condition, it would be easiest to treat him at our center. They consented to let us take him for a week. The director at the center shared that in March or April of 2006, he had found Zachariah in a garbage bag behind a building across the street from his center. This little boy who was thrown away was not unnoticed by God. Not only was he lifted out of the garbage (literally!), but now he was being placed in the care of our center.

(October 17th, 2006)

Because Zachariah is on medicine and needs high maintenance, I was asked to have him sleep in my house so I could care for him and keep up on his medications. So I have gained a son for a week! During the day when I have lots of work, he can sit in his stroller in the girls' area with the tias. I am giving him various medicine at the appropriate times, bathing him in the morning and evening with a special antibacterial treatment, and using a spray to treat the scabies, feeding him his meals, changing his diapers, and loving on him! The girls think he is wonderful, and they all want to push him around in his stroller. He laughs and smiles while they do!

* * *

He was a precious little fellow. His ear infection would keep him up at night. I would wake to him crying and would carry him back and forth across the room in my arms, trying to get him to stop crying and go to sleep.

After a week, it was decided that he would be with us indefinitely. The little boys' dorm was pretty full and had a few special-needs children who occupied those tias' time. It was decided it would be best to have him sleep in the head tia's room in the girls' dorm, so he could have the attention and care he needed. He was soon sitting up on his own, and the girls loved to play "mommy" to him. He didn't talk but loved to smile. His ear infection was not going away, and there was always puss oozing out of one ear. The poor little guy had been suffering so much. After a few rounds of antibiotics, without it getting better, he was taken for an exam at the hospital. There they found and removed two dead flies from his ear. After that, he quickly healed up.

In spring of 2008, my dad and sister came to visit. A physical therapist friend sent leg braces along with them for Zachariah. We started using them right away and doing therapy to strengthen Zachariah's body so he would be able to stand. In 2011, my dad, our PT friend and I visited Mozambique, and Zachariah had made so much progress! He was walking with assistance and feeding himself. Zachariah was living in what was (at the time) a house for some of the little boys. Our PT friend showed the caregivers some more exercises they could do to help Zachariah. Now Zachariah is able to walk all by himself!! What a joy it has been to see God lift this little boy from the rubbish and give him a new life! He was thrown out and left as worthless. But to God, this little boy was worth it. He has value and purpose, and God is changing his life! Not only that, but getting to watch Zachariah grow has been a joy to those who have had the privilege of caring for him. It has taken a lot of time and effort, but it is well worth it to everyone who has had a part in his life!

We received several other children over time from that center. Over time the conditions of that center improved considerably.

Chapter 8

Lessons

Part 1 – "Don't Speed Skate"

I had a dream one night. I was out on an ice rink, wearing ice skates and a pretty ice skating outfit, dancing with Jesus. The lights were low, and I didn't see all of the people in the seats watching. It was just Jesus and myself dancing in perfect harmony, and it was beautiful. Suddenly lights went on, and I saw a crowded room. Two people came skating toward me, saying "Come on! Hurry! It's time for speed skating!" and they picked me up so I was sitting on their arms, one on each side of me. My legs were sticking straight out, and they were racing across the ice to get me ready for the speed skating. I was confused and didn't know why this was happening. As they were going, my legs were running into other skaters on the ice and knocking them over. When we reached the edge, they set me down and handed me speed skates, trying to make me hurry along. The atmosphere went from beauty and harmony and peace, to chaos and confusion. Then I woke up, and right away, I felt the Lord speak to me, *"Don't speed skate."*

It is far too easy to get caught up with the things that need to be done, that we can speed skate along in the race, and miss the dance. God has called us to live out of a place of rest in Him. There are so many things that can pull us in a thousand directions, and sometimes we can even knock others down or not take time with people, because we have lost our focus and are rushing along. I don't want to speed skate; I do want to ice dance. I want to be in such harmony with the Lord that He is my one focus. All that I do will flow out of being with Jesus.

Part 2 – "Martha was Distracted"

I have a confession. I never really understood the story of Mary and Martha. I identified with Martha. For goodness' sake, *somebody* had to do the work if they were going to have dinner! Jesus said, "Mary chose what was better" because she sat at His feet. But come on! Martha was working hard and serving and getting things done. What was wrong with that? One morning, my Bible reading included that story. "Lord, help me to understand *why* what Mary did was better," I prayed. I read it again, and this time something jumped out at me that hadn't before: *Martha was **distracted** by all of the preparations that needed to be made.*

There are lots of really good things I can do, but if it distracts me from God, it is not worth doing! This was a new lesson God was about to teach me.

I was busy. There was always something to do, and I began measuring the success of my day by how many things I had accomplished. The more I did in a day, the better the day was. If I hadn't accomplished many things, the day wasn't that fruitful.

I would lie in bed at night with a running list going through my head of all I had done that day. This had been going on and becoming more of an obsession for a few weeks, when one day I was walking to the market to buy fruit. Along the way, I was going over in my mind all of the things I had done so far that day, counting up for my personal productivity meter. *I have sorted the new donations for the girls, taken clothes to be mended by the sewing lady, cleaned the house, made snacks for the HIV girls, fed Gilda, worked on the girls' files, and am now going to the market, and it's not even twelve o'clock! This is a great day...*

Then a familiar, quiet voice broke through my thoughts with, "Anna, I am not counting." "Lord," I said, "if you are not counting, then *why* am I counting?" In His gracious way, the Lord showed me that my measure of success has nothing to do with how many items I can tick off a list, or how many accomplishments I have. The measure of success is really, "Did I glorify God, and do what He asked me to do?"

A few days later, I had brought back beans and rice from the kitchen and was heading back to my room to eat lunch. In the missionary compound, my Mozambican friend was sitting down on an esteira (caniso reed mat) to eat her own lunch. I decided to join her, and we enjoyed each other's company and small talk. But in my mind, I was still running through all of the things I should get done that day, so as I finished eating, I was about to excuse myself. Then I felt the Lord speak to me, "This is the most important thing you could be doing today. You can get up and go, but you will miss this."

I chose to stay put (what else could I do?), and the next thing I knew, my friend was pouring her heart out to me. Her job at the center was cleaning the short-term compound—from raking the leaves on the ground, to washing the bedding and cleaning the toilets. She shared with me her testimony of how she used to work at a bank. She used to look down on the lady who cleaned the toilets at the bank, thinking she did not have a very important job. "Now I am cleaning toilets. Now I realize that whatever God gives us to do is important. Somebody has to clean the toilets just as much as somebody needs to work at computers! Whatever we do, we should do it for God." I was so humbled – humbled by her sharing this amazing story, and humbled that I could have missed it if I had chosen to go do other things "more important" than sitting here enjoying fellowship with my friend.

The Lord's message to me was clear, and I think of it so often! He has taught me to settle down; He has taught me to take time; to not rush along; to not speed skate. When I am in tune with Him, I get to see amazing things happen. I can take time to pray for someone, I can sit down to drink tea with a friend in the middle of the day, and not feel guilty thinking of all of the things I still have to do. I can live with purpose and live out of Christ. When I am in tune with Him, I am not distracted by all of the things that need to be done. And somehow, the things that need to be done still get done. But I am not under pressure that, if they don't get done, I have failed. Now my goal (and I daily have to make it this) is to do what I feel God wants me to do. Jesus said He does only what He sees the Father doing. I want to be in such harmony with the Lord that I do only what I see Him doing!

Chapter 9
The Day of the Bombs

It was March 22nd, 2007, the day after my 21st birthday. We had had such a fun evening the night before, as all of the missionaries gathered for home group in one of the missionaries' backyards. They had decorated for my birthday, and we had dinner together, and they prayed for me.

I sat on my wicker chair, early this Thursday morning, reading my Bible. Today I read Psalm 91. The day continued with working on various things for the girls, then meeting with Ellie to pray before we had discipleship with the older girls. We had been specifically talking about and praying for one of the new girls who was from a Muslim family. We were praying that she would understand God's love for her and accept Jesus as her Savior. At 3:00, we invited the girls in for our weekly discipleship program. That day, we clearly presented the Gospel to them. We were having such a good time that we went longer than the usual hour. At 4:30, we dismissed the girls so they could shower before supper. Ellie and I could hear what sounded like thunder in the distance and stepped outside to see where the storm was coming from, but the sky was clear and blue – not a cloud to be seen. *That's strange!* We went out of the short-term compound to the playground area to check out what was going on and to get a better view of the direction the noise was coming from.

On the playground, many of the children and adults had gathered and were watching across the wall where smoke was rising in the distance. It seemed to be coming from the arms depot about a mile away from our center. The booming was growing more frequent, and one of the missionaries, George, said, "We don't have to worry unless missiles start to fly." I made sure all of the girls were out of the girls' dorm "just in case." I wasn't exactly worried about anything really dangerous happening, but thought it was responsible to keep all of the girls together. I thought I would run over to the baby house just to see how the babies and toddlers were handling the noise. Reaching the baby house, I climbed the steps to the doorway. Just as I was about to enter inside, a huge blast that shook the ground exploded from the arms depot. It was described later as a mushroom bomb. The rafters rattled, and dust and pieces fell from the ceiling. Windows around the center shattered, and children were screaming. I picked up the baby closest to me, grabbed the hand of a toddler, and I along with everyone else at the center took off running. Someone had shouted that we should run toward the soccer field at the front of the center. That seemed strange to me because I thought we should seek shelter, not go for an open space. Many of the children and missionaries and workers made it to the soccer field, but those of us with smaller children we were carrying were a bit slower. Suddenly, shrapnel started landing on the soccer field, and missiles were flying overhead. Those who had made it to the soccer field first took off through the center gate, running for their lives. Some ran into the fields across the street and lay low in the brush, some were taken in by neighbors. Some climbed on transportation buses and were driven far away from the direction of the arms depot. Those of us who had not yet arrived at the soccer field quickly changed direction. We ran for the prayer hut. We stood outside for a minute, not sure if we were safer inside or out. Some of us began calling out loud to the Lord with all our might. When missiles flew very close over our heads, we flooded into the prayer hut. Some of the pastors started duct-taping the windows, so if they would break, they would not shatter on us. We all found a spot on the floor to sit. I had three-year old João in between my legs and a toddler sitting on each leg.

I wanted to try to call my family, and when the call went through, my sister Cara answered the phone. I didn't want to tell her at first that bombs were exploding. I cried out over the phone, "Pray Cara! Pray like you have never prayed before!" The connection was lost, and I felt bad that I had to leave the call like that. The grass roof on the prayer hut was being redone and was not complete in the middle. Through the lengthwise opening across the center of the roof, we could see missiles flying through the sky. The prayer hut was on the edge of the center (the furthermost area on the center from the arms depot). The missiles were whistling and screaming through the air, then everything would go quiet and we would wait for the explosion. The ground would shake, and our bodies trembled. One of the pastors began singing a chorus of "Alleluia." Then he began another song, and we joined in singing with all of our voices, "Jesus passando por aqui." Translated, the song is, "Jesus is passing by, Jesus is passing by. And as He passes, everything is transformed. Sorrow must flee; joy has come." During this song, a missile whistled overhead and exploded on the other side of the wall to the center. As we were huddled together in the prayer hut, I could not stop praying out loud. Whenever I stopped praying out loud, I felt overcome with fear and had to start praying again. I was worried about the girls who had run off the center and was trying to take a tally to see who was with us and who was missing. I felt certain that I would die that night. I remember a feeling of peace about dying. I knew I was where the Lord had called me, and I knew my family knew I loved them. I was ready. I remember praying, "Lord, I know you have plans for my life and you have told me things you want me to do. But if, at this moment, you have changed those plans and I am going to die, I am ready to go." In the midst of this terror going on around us, I had such a peace in my heart, realizing that I was not afraid to die.

Ellie's husband, Alex, was gathered with a group of people taking shelter behind a school building. Ellie talked to him on the phone and said that he thought if one group was hit, then not everyone would be killed if we were in two groups. I was horrified at the thought of one group dying and the rest living and thought *I want to be with the group that dies, because I don't think I could bear the pain of losing so many friends, and myself surviving.*

One of the missionary nurses decided to make a run for the baby house to get the medicine for the children who were HIV positive and needed their medication at specific times. While she was on her way back to the prayer hut, with her basket of medicine in one hand and her camera in the other, a missile flew very low and very near her head. She was unharmed.

The bombs and missiles continued for four-and-a-half hours. As it grew dark, the moon rose and shone in through the roof. I saw the moon and thought *How could the moon have the nerve to shine on a night like this? How could anything go on as normal on a night like this?*

Finally, everything grew quiet. The whistling screams of the missiles faded, the rumbling explosions stopped. We waited, not sure if it was truly over. Some of the older boys went to the kitchen and carried back large pots of rice and sauce that the kitchen workers had prepared earlier, and we fed the children a late supper in the prayer hut.

We decided that it had been quiet long enough; that it would be safe to venture out of our shelter. I walked with the girls back to their dorm, and we were all still trembling and feeling nervous. Together we assessed the damage of the dorm—mostly broken windows and a few split beams on the ceilings, and some rooms had holes in the ceiling where shrapnel had fallen through. In a couple of rooms, the light fixtures had fallen from the ceiling and shattered on the floor. My own apartment door was wide open. The shaking had caused the door to break away from the frame so it would only stay shut if the deadbolt was locked. Dust and bits of wood had fallen from the ceiling beams, settling all over the floor and furniture. Around 9 o'clock p.m. all of my girls—except for three—came back. We got all of the girls to bed. Some slept on the floor of other girls' rooms. I went to another missionary's house. I was too shaken up to sleep alone. I was finally able to reach my parents by phone, and they were relieved to hear that we were okay and that I was alive. Part of me had wondered if they would want me to return home right away thinking it was too dangerous for me to be there. But my dad calmed those silent worries by saying, "We were sure you would be okay. But even if you had died, we know you are where God wants you, and that is the best place to be."

It was hard to sleep that night, processing in my mind all that had just gone on, and still not sure if it was really over.

The following morning the other three girls returned, and all of the boys came back. I walked with some Mozambicans and Ellie around the center to see what damage had been done. The church/dining hall windows were shattered, and a missile or bomb had fallen through the ceiling and part of the wall at the corner of the stage. One of the missionaries, who taught in the Bible school, told the students who were waiting for their class to start to get out of the Bible school. They did, and the Bible school was hit after they left. Something had exploded at the car park but did no damage to the vehicles parked there. It seemed that the center had been majorly hit about five times, and many more times than we could count from falling shrapnel.

It is nothing but a miracle that none of our children, workers or missionaries were killed or injured. God protected us! Some of our workers started coming back from their own homes, saying all their neighbors' houses were flattened, but theirs just had broken glass. The neighbors had been killed or had lost limbs, but those from Iris Ministries had walked away without a scratch.

Late Friday morning, the police were worried the explosions might start up again and asked for everyone to evacuate. We loaded up all the girls, baby house children, and youngest boys on trucks and took them to another Iris Ministries' center in Machava, about 40 minutes away. Along the way we could see more damage done. The psychiatric hospital down the road had been hit many times and now had shattered windows and several huge holes in the large building. Several of the people there had died. The gas station was hit through the front window—but amazingly, the gas pumps were not. It was sad to see so many Mozambicans, with all the possessions they could carry on their backs, walking on foot to evacuate.

We returned home with the children that evening when the police felt it was safe for people to return to their homes.

On the educator shift change day, all of the dorm parents from the previous shift went home, some still unsure how their families were. The new shift came on. The head tia for the girls' dorm was a wreck. I wrapped my arms around her and she cried, and then told me she and her children were lying against a wall, and four of her neighbors who were sitting against the same wall lost their lives in an explosion. It was horrible! She and her children were untouched.

The children who had fled the center shared stories of their experience. Some were running for their lives and witnessed people being hit by missiles. Others had missiles zoom close to them but were not even touched. They shared how kind neighbors took them in and fed them. The Lord took care of each one.

With all of the terrible things that happened that night, God kept us safe under the shelter of His wings. We met death face-to-face and walked away unharmed. God is perfect, and His ways we cannot always understand, but He is faithful to His people. We *lived* Psalm 91.

My Grandparents phoned me the day after to see if we were all okay, and I was so glad to hear their voices! It really blessed me that they would call to check up on me.

One day several of us missionaries and Mozambicans went into the village behind our center to visit families, pray for them and see what damage had been done in our community. It was sad to see the destruction caused by those missiles. As we visited one family, they showed us how one missile had gone through a block wall, through their house and a few other homes, drifted upward, going through another wall, and then took off to find a new place to destroy. This family had been in their home when the missile tore through the walls right beside them! Several people we visited had been wounded, were missing limbs, or were now in wheelchairs or on crutches. We prayed for those we met, prayed for healing for them emotionally, and prayed for peace in our community.

The next days, weeks, even months after the explosions, I think many of us experienced post-traumatic stress disorder. A few days afterwards, Ellie and I were sitting in my room talking, and a visitor who had arrived after the events took place started banging on his new drum from the souvenir market. With each beat of the drum, I had shivers run up my spine, and my heart would start racing. Finally, we had to ask him kindly to please stop and explained why. When doors would slam shut, the same feeling would come over me. I just wanted to crawl under a bed and hide.

The children would play outside and reenact with their toy airplanes the missiles flying through the air. I hated hearing them whistle, mimicking the whistle of the missiles screaming through the air on that horrible night. Even though I knew it was the children this time, my first feeling before I could think was fear.

One night several weeks after the explosions, I went out to eat with some of the missionaries. As we sat chatting in the restaurant, the wind was picking up outside. I wondered if I was the only one who was having a hard time concentrating because the sound of the wind was so similar to the rumble of the bombs. Then Ellie mentioned she was hearing it too, and we wondered how long it would be before the noises wouldn't bother us so much.

The first storm that came after the explosions was very loud. The girls were hiding out in their bedrooms, and I went up to the baby house to see how the toddlers were handling the booming thunder noises. Some of them were crying, and some were carrying on as normal. Little João—who I had carried from the baby house during the explosions—came running up to me and, taking my hand, said, "Mana Anna, let's sing 'Jesus passando por aqui.'" He remembered the peace that came as we sang that song during the explosions, and now I sang it quietly with him as the Lord swept away the fear in his little heart caused by the storm and brought peace again to him. Knowing that God is in control of the storm and is perfectly capable of sheltering us in His strong hands makes it a lot easier to walk through the storm.

As I walked back through the visitors' compound after the storm had subsided, I looked up in the sky, and there was the most amazing rainbow I had ever seen. The colors were so brilliant, and the rainbow stretched out from one end of our children's center to the other. It was a reminder of God's promise to Noah, sealed with a rainbow, that he would never flood the whole earth again. I had been living in such fear that the explosions could start up again at any time. The Lord showed me (and all the others who saw it and were also in awe of the Lord's promise!) that He would protect us, and the explosions would not start up again.

This was tested when, a few weeks later, we started hearing bombs exploding off in the distance. It didn't seem to be coming from the same direction as before, but it was certainly bombs exploding. One, two, three… We waited and wondered what was going on. My heart sank. I prayed *Lord, I am going home to see my family in just a few weeks! Please spare me so I can see them!* Again, I felt him remind me that He had made a promise to me and that He does not go back on His promises. Later we learned that we had indeed heard bombs exploding. As a matter of fact, they were finally doing what should have been done years ago by removing the ammo to a 'safe' place to detonate it. About once a week after that, they would detonate three bombs. Each time I would stop to count, and wait to be sure. Each time it started (we were never warned when they were going to do it) I felt my whole body go limp with fear, but I held on to God's promise. He did not go back on His promise—and for the record, He *never* goes back on His promises!

At the end of May, I boarded a plane and headed home for a ten-week visit with my lovely family. It was so wonderful and emotional to hug my mom, dad and siblings, and be with them after not being sure I would ever see them again.

CHAPTER 10

Mothering

For as long as I can remember, I have had one constant desire: to mother children. I played mommy to my dolls when I was little, I played mommy to my younger siblings, and I loved to hold other people's babies. I remember when my mom would be expecting, I would play with my dolls and imagine that they were the real baby, but it just didn't compare to taking care of *real* children. I started babysitting officially when I was eleven years old. By the time I was thirteen years old my Friday and Saturday nights were always booked babysitting for different families, as well as a few babysitting jobs during the week. I loved that and the opportunity it gave me to learn the responsibilities of caring for children and of being a mom.

When I moved to Africa, I had such a burden to be a mother to children who did not have one—whether because of death, illness that kept the mother from caring properly for her child, or simply the absence of a caring, nurturing mother. It was easy to be mama to the babies and toddlers in the baby house. They were cute, loved you back, and just thrived on attention. They needed discipline at times, but often because they didn't know better yet. They were just learning.

The girls (ages four to eighteen) were also easy to love—for the most part. But there were times, as I'm sure every parent must experience, when it was not so easy to love the girls. The Lord taught me a lot through being a dorm mother.

I had not been there for very long when a few of the older girls began testing me. They were very rude and told me things like, "You should just go back to America where you belong," and in general had bad attitudes (I will not say "teenage" attitudes, because not all teens go through that stage!). I struggled along and did not feel loving toward these girls at all. When the girls would knock, if I knew that one of the particularly difficult girls was batting at my door, I would cringe and already put up a guard of how to respond before I even opened the door. One day as I was praying for the girls, the Lord revealed to me my own heart's attitude. He showed me, "Anna, you are loving these girls conditionally. If they are being nice and kind, you love them, but if they are being bitter or disrespectful, you stop loving them. You love them under the conditions that they behave properly, but when they don't, you stop loving them." It was true! I was loving them conditionally. I prayed about that for several days, asking the Lord to change my heart and give me a heart like His that loves unconditionally. That doesn't make the way they are behaving okay, but it does say I love *you* and care about *you*, and I don't want you to behave this way, but you are, and I still love you and care about you. I know there is tough love, and that the Lord disciplines those He loves. The fact is, He still loves us! While we were yet sinners, Christ died for us. God demonstrated His own love for us through sending

His Son to us when we were disrespectful, bitter, rude sinners. And for those who will come to Him, He has paid the pardon for our sins, so that we could have abundant life through Him!

A few years after this, when I was living in the United States again, I had an argument with my dad. I don't remember what it was about, but afterward I felt ashamed and went to my dad's room to ask for forgiveness. He did forgive me and gave me a hug. When he hugged me I had a realization that *I* also need to be loved unconditionally! I found it hard to live with some of the girls, but I am not so easy to live with either! I need that unconditional love graced on me! It was a beautiful and overwhelming realization, and through my dad loving me it revealed to me God's love for me.

In Mozambique, it is modest and proper for the women and girls to wear skirts or dresses to church. Some of our girls were not keeping up with washing their own clothes, so on Sunday mornings, they would wear jeans to church. I talked with some of the Mozambican dorm mothers, and they felt it was disrespectful for the girls to dress like that when they were going to church and that they should be wearing their best. I agreed, so we talked to all of the girls and told them that they had all week to do their washing, so on Sundays, they should have clean skirts for church. On Friday and on Saturday, we reminded the girls to do their washing so they would have clean clothes for Sunday. Sunday morning, I walked into the girls' dorm, and each of the girls had on fresh and clean skirts or dresses. They looked lovely and happy. Then out of one of the rooms came one of the younger teens. She was wearing jeans that were not clean, and she had a bit of *what are you going to do about it?* attitude. I told her she needed to go put on a capalana (wrap skirt). She told me all of her clothes were dirty. I told her she had been repeatedly reminded to wash her clothes, so there was no reason that they should be dirty. If they were, she would just have to put on a dirty skirt. "No—that would be embarrassing!" she retorted. "Well, that is your fault," I said, "you should have thought of that yesterday when you were told to wash your clothes." The point here was going beyond the skirt, and to rebellion in her heart. We told her that if she arrived at church without a skirt on, we would have to walk her back to the dorm to put one on.

I really hoped she would listen. As everyone was arriving at church and taking their seats, in trotted our girl with jeans. She took her seat on the bench and glanced at me to see what I would do. It was not convenient, and it was not fun, but I had to follow through. I told her to come with me. She finally got up and followed me back to the girls' dorm. In her room, I searched through her clothes and could not find anything that looked clean. Finally, I grabbed one of the other girls' skirts and told her to borrow it just for church. At this point, she blew up. She burst into tears and cried out, "You cannot tell me what to do! You are not my mother!" Those words were like a blow to my heart. I wanted to be her mother and loved her like she was my daughter. I hated to discipline her, but I cared more about her character than about letting her get away with this. I felt a lump in my throat, but I said to her, "I am not your mother, but God has put me here to take care of you. You have to obey." She put on the skirt and stormed off to church. I went to my room and cried. When I could compose myself, I returned to church.

The next day, she came knocking at my door for something she wanted. I found what she needed and gave it to her. She stood there in the doorway, took what I handed her, and looking me in the eyes, she said gently, "Thank you, Mama." I smiled so big at her. She may not have asked for forgiveness or said she was sorry, but she showed what was truly in her heart by calling me "Mama." Something changed in our relationship that day. And I believe God *did* use me to be the mom she so desperately needed during that season of her life.

Two of our girls struggled a lot in school. Neither of them could read or write, but as they had been passed along in grades, they would sit in class or sleep because they were not able to participate with the children who could read or write. They would proudly bring me their report cards or their tests—not realizing that the big red letters showed that they had failed. We worked with the girls, but the improvement was slow. Even though they could not read, they had learned to write a few words. They could write their own names, and from all of the English-speaking missionaries, they had learned to write, "I love you" in English and in Portuguese. Every day, the siren would sound to announce the close of the school day. Soon you would hear lots of children running to their dorms. Several times a week as the stampede of kiddos would run into the girls' dorm, a little piece of paper would be slipped under my door from one of the two girls. It would be covered with sweet drawings of princesses and flowers and hearts, and would say "Mana Anna, eu te amo. I love Mana Anna. Mana Anna loves [Insert name]."

These little notes and cards were treasures to me. While the girls sat bored in class, they would create a little piece of art on a torn-out notebook page and be thinking of me. It really made my day, and I saved many of those sweet notes.

Quality Time
(Blog journal entry)

I am always trying to find ways to have quality time with the girls. Sometimes it is easier to just do things myself, but asking a few girls to come help me gives them the opportunity to learn, and for us to have quality time together. With 50 girls in the dorm, it's not always easy to spread out quality time with each one.

Every Friday night, I do a snack and movie night in the girls' dorm. I usually give them something healthy (hard-boiled eggs, popcorn, fruit, peanut butter). Sometimes I make them cookies or cupcakes. Last week, two of the newer girls helped me prepare peanut butter on crackers for all the girls. They were so impressed with our kitchen – refrigerators, a stove and oven, plates, cups and silverware. "Mana Anna, you have everything in this kitchen! Plates, cups! You thought of everything!" One exclaimed when she walked into our kitchen and took a look around her. The other pointed to an apple on one of the other missionaries' shelves and said, "You even have an apple in here!" ☺ Now compared to America, our kitchen is pretty basic. I mean, we just had a small countertop built in, but have been surviving for a few years with just a stove, sink, fridge and table. But these girls have probably only ever seen a cooking pot over a wood fire, and a few mismatched plates to eat off of! They both came from pretty poor circumstances. It was a reminder to me where they came from, and how much it is for them to take in all that we have here! Even having beds, instead of sleeping on grass mats on the floor, must be a big deal to them.

They spread peanut butter on 50 crackers, and even washed up the plates and knives afterwards. All the while they laughed and talked and shared stories about the places they lived before coming to our center. I got to learn more of their backgrounds and see their individual personalities and abilities.

Sometimes I can get really busy doing "good things" but neglect the whole point I am here—to be a mother to these precious girls, and to show them God's love. God has been reminding me to take time to create special moments for the girls. And as I bless them, I feel so blessed.

* * *

From Rags to Riches

"A Father to the fatherless, a defender of widows, is God in His holy dwelling. God sets the lonely in families…"
Psalm 68:5-6a

Melina came to us from the police station. The police found this little girl—about seven years old—roaming the streets. She was sick, so they took her to the hospital and then they brought her to our center. I would usually let the new girls take a shower in my bathroom, and I would pick out a few new clothes for them. Ellie and some of the girls would usually come to help the new girl feel welcome. Then we would pray with her, show her to her new room, and introduce her to the tias. It was fun to welcome in the new girls, and precious to pray with them for the first time.

The first day Melina arrived, she was a wild little thing. We bathed her in a nice, hot shower. It was her first shower ever, and she was a little skeptical of getting into the shower with this hot water pouring out. We found dresses to fit her in the donated clothes. We prayed with her. Then Ellie and I said we were going to take her out to meet the tias. Melina threw herself down on the floor and did not want to leave my room. She tried to bite me when I started getting her to stand up. Finally we coaxed her out the door, and introduced her to the tias. They greeted her warmly, and we showed her where she would get to sleep.

Later that evening, I went into the girls' dorm to check in on our new little arrival, and to see how things were going in the dorm. As I was walking in the dark back to my room, Melina came running up to me, and, taking my hand, began walking along side me. "I am going to sleep with you tonight!" She informed me cheerfully. "No," I responded, "you have to sleep here in the girls' dorm." She had already made her mind up that she would sleep with me, so she pouted and hung onto my arm.

The next morning, the tia who slept in Melina's room was very tired. "Melina was literally hanging from the rafters!" She told us. She would climb from the top bunk bed to hang from the beams on the ceiling. She would not sleep during the night, but during the day she would lie down on a mat and sleep for several hours.

Coming from the streets she must have stayed awake all night long to protect herself. Now she was in the habit of sleeping through the day. Over time, our little, wild girl settled down and became quite sweet and thoughtful.

When new girls arrived Melina loved to come in and assist us in picking out new clothes for them. She would recall with thoughtfulness her first warm shower and how special it was to get new clothes. She would help the new girls settle in, and was so friendly and kind. She had a fun and outgoing personality, and I felt like I could always tell what she was thinking by the expression on her face.

Maria came with her brother. Maria was shy at first, especially of me being white. But she quickly warmed up to our joyful girls. She rarely called me "Mana Anna" as the other girls did. She would always call me "Mama." It made me feel sad that she was not with her real mother, but I was honored to fill that role, along with the other ladies who worked in the girls' dorm.

Fina came when she was about seven years old. She also came with her little brother. Their mother abandoned them, and their father was abusive. Social services brought the children to us.

When a new child arrived, we would take them to the clinic for a well check-up (or sick check-up, depending on the child). We took Fina to the clinic, and she was very nervous about the white missionaries. The missionary nurse went to pat her on the head, and little Fina winced when she saw the nurse's hand raised. She was so used to abuse that she was expecting to be hit. I felt so sorry for her, and was so grateful God had brought her out of the nasty home she had been in and to our center.

It took some time for Fina to get settled in at the center. She was very loving towards her little brother, and whenever the children were out on the playground, she would make sure she was with her brother to protect him. She would look out for him, and make sure he was fed well (all of the children were fed well!), and sometimes she would save some of her bread from breakfast to give to him.

Fina loved coming to our little girls' discipleship program on Friday afternoons. I remember praying about her in desperation, "Lord, how can we explain to someone who has been sexually abused by her earthly father, that you are a loving father?! How could she know what a loving father is like?" Then one day, Fina came and said to me, "Mana Anna, I felt Jesus come to me and tell me to sit on His lop. I felt He told me he brought me to the center because He loves me and wants to protect me and take care of me."

That is just how our loving Father is! The Lord personally showed her what a loving Father He is.

Fina was always full of questions about God. She would pray from her heart, and she would often start conversations with the other girls about God. Many times, a group of little girls would come to me, always including Fina, to ask questions or talk to me about God.

One night, I was sitting in the girls' dorm. They were watching a movie, but three of the girls came to sit with me. They asked me about Heaven and what Heaven was like. I told them that God is preparing a place for each one of us, and one day when He is ready He will take us to be with Him there. One of the girls asked, "Can we go there now?" I smiled at her eagerness, and told her we would go when God wanted us to.

Just as I was writing this, I realized that one of those girls was Helena (who used to pass notes and drawings under my door after school). In 2011, while I was back in Mozambique for a visit with my dad and our friend, Greg, little Helena (who was eleven at the time) was quite sick. She had a terrible headache, and the hospital kept sending her back to the center. One evening at church my dad prayed for her. The next day as I was walking to the kitchen to get bread, she came running up alongside me and, taking my hand, she said, "Mana Anna! I am feeling better today. Your dad prayed for me last night, and God made me feel better! It is because your dad prayed for me."

Sweet Helena was always quick to pray for things and to recognize God's responding to our prayers.

But her headaches came back. We have a picture that our friend took a few nights before we left. Dad is sitting on a bench in the girls' dorm, holding and comforting Helena who was feeling very sick. He was being a daddy to a little girl who did not have an earthly dad to care for her. The day after we left to go home to the United States, Helena was back in the hospital, was diagnosed with meningitis, and died.

Helena was such a huge part of the girls' dorm. She was bursting with personality. She always wanted to hold my hand, and always had something to share with me about her day. I had known her since she was a baby in the baby house, had taught her preschool and how to write her name, and was privileged along with others to be a mother to her. And I was privileged to have conversations with her such as the one we had the night we talked about Heaven. Helena is there now, where she could only imagine with great anticipation what it would be like. I write this with tears in my eyes. Our sweet girl is in Heaven, and one day, when God is ready, I will see her there.

After Helena passed away, Ellie e-mailed me. She remembered that so many weekends when other girls were going to go visit family, Helena would get her things ready and wait in hopes that her grandmother would come to take her for a visit. Her grandmother rarely came. Helena would tell us that her grandmother was coming for her and that they were going to bake a cake or cookies together and have a party. When Ellie heard that Helena passed away, she felt God give her a picture of Helena in Heaven having the party she had always longed for!

I can only imagine what it will be like, but I know that God has something wonderful awaiting us. This life is quickly passing, and I want to make it count. And I know that this is not all I have to look forward to. We who know Christ as our Savior get to look forward, with great expectation and anticipation, to what God has prepared for us on the other side of this life.

The Reading Program
(Blog journal entry)

About fifteen months ago we started a reading program. Many of the girls and boys, even up to fifth grade, cannot read. They did not catch on in first grade, so they were passed to second and third and so on without any extra attention. Or they started school late but, because of their age, were put straight into a class without assessing their abilities. Then in school they do a lot of repeating what the teacher says back to him, or copying off the chalkboard. But not so much mental work so it is easy to slide along without ever learning to read. This is the problem we discovered.

Ellie, one of the tias and I began testing all of the girls to see where they were at. If they could read fourth grade books or better, they were fine. Some could only read a few easy words, and some didn't even know their vowels, let alone the whole alphabet. We wanted to work with those girls who struggled, so they could learn to read well.

After testing them, the tias worked with the girls in the afternoons with chalkboards, paper and pencils, books, and flash cards. Some of them still struggle, but many of them have improved so much! In September I started volunteering in the school (we have a school for the children who live here and children from the community. They teach preschool through seventh grade.), and now I am working with forty fourth graders on Thursday and Friday mornings, teaching them to read.

I feel that God has really given me some strategies. Sometimes I will be praying, and an idea pops into my head. Or I'll be lying in bed and start getting creative plans for how to teach these kids. Last week I was playing "Memory" with some of the girls and thought *I should make a memory game with the letters of the alphabet!* I made one on the computer, printed it out on pink paper, cut the letters out in squares, and laminated the cards. The kids in the school love it. They get to play a game, and don't even realize how much they are learning. It has been great because so many of them haven't learned the alphabet, and I have been struggling how to teach it to them so that it would stick in their minds and they would 'get it.' They are learning the letters and matching them. They are learning to memorize by remembering where the card are placed. They are learning to see small differences, like the difference between 'b' and 'd' and 'p'. It's been so good for them.

It's exciting when you are teaching a child, and suddenly something "clicks" in their mind, and they get it! They are so thrilled and proud of themselves. It's a privilege to be a part of it.

* * *

Chapter 11

Mice, Spiders and Snakes!!

I have a few phobias. One is a terrible fear of mice. So when I began hearing a mouse scuffing around my house at night, I was quite scared. One day, I pulled out a brand new box of oatmeal, only to find a hole had been chewed out of it and mouse droppings inside. I was disgusted. I put everything that was not in a can into my refrigerator. Even my plastic box with a lid that I kept spices and things in was chewed on. One night, I had a few missionaries over to watch a movie. We heard a scratching noise, and then saw mouse run across my floor. We all screamed and ran out of the house. A few of the visitors woke from the noise we had made and came running to see what was wrong. We felt bad for making such a fuss over a mouse. I borrowed a cat for a night, but he didn't do the job I intended for him to do.

One of the missionaries set a mousetrap for me, and I was thrilled to find the mouse dead one day when I came in the door. I had to have a missionary fellow come dispose of it for me, and I thought I was finally free! And I was… for a few nights. Then, as I lay in bed trying to sleep, I heard the scratching sound again. Only this time it was close – too close. A wretched mouse was scratching around UNDER MY BED! I had the mosquito net tucked in tight under my mattress – something I did every night, not so much to keep the mosquitos away (although for that, too!), but so no critters could join me in bed. I made a mad dash out of my bed and I think I crossed the six feet of floor from my bed to the front room in one giant leap. I shut the door and stuffed pillow cases underneath so the mouse could not come through the crack. I had a hard time sleeping that night, wondering what the mouse was destroying and feeling violated that it had come into my house. In the morning, the pillowcases had holes in them from the mouse trying to chew his way out of my room. More mousetraps were set, but the mouse was getting smart. I began to realize he was probably not the only mouse. Rat poison was set out, and slowly I began finding dead mice. I was so grateful for the missionary fellows who kindly disposed of the mice as we found them. One of my missionary friends offered to help me clean out the large cupboards in my front room that were used for storage for the girls' dorm. They were full of clothing and shoe donations, craft supplies, toiletries, tools and gifts. We started pulled everything out, searching carefully for any critters. In the end, we found ten dead mice, including a few babies in a shoebox. I was so horrified, and my missionary friend finally said, "Anna, just go! You can't help me in this state, so I will take care of it. I am not afraid of them." I felt bad leaving her to do the job, but I was grateful for her help because I truly could not handle it.

One evening I filled up a plastic box with water and some yummy-smelling foot scrub I had picked up in South Africa. When you wear flip flops and walk around in the sand all the time, it feels so nice to clean up your feet, especially before going to bed, so you don't have sand in the sheets. I soaked my feet and enjoyed a little spa treatment, while reading a book and journaling. It was pretty late, and I stepped out onto a towel I had laid on the floor (so I wouldn't be stepping with my clean feet on the sandy floor). I was about to take the water to dump in the bathroom sink, when there on the floor in the doorway to the bathroom was a very large yellow and gray spider. I was so frightened. I wanted to call Alex and Ellie, who were living in the room next door to mine, to come help me, but it was very late, and I would have to step right beside the spider to get to my phone. I stood there filled with fear and could feel tears coming to my eyes and a lump in my throat. Then I realized *I am being overcome with fear by a creature I am much bigger than, and that God created. I can overcome this!* So I said, "I command you to go in Jesus' name!" And just like that, it was gone! I didn't see it crawl away. I had a large stack of blankets I had brought in from the girls because the weather was no longer cool enough for them. I had washed and folded them, and they were in the corner right by where the spider had been. But the spider had not gone into them. It was just gone! I know God sent it away. It was a good lesson for me to learn, that we can stand in the authority God has given us through His Holy Spirit and don't have to be overcome by fear. Even if it was just a spider (a great big, ugly, probably poisonous spider...), it helps me to be even more confident in Him for bigger things.

On occasion, we came across snakes at the center. Often they were at the back of the center in the open area where the children rarely played. One Thursday evening, however, we had an uninvited visitor in the girls' dorm. The girls were returning from the Thursday evening church service. One of the girls said she saw a snake. Ellie and I went to inspect, but all we could find was a rippling path in the sand that certainly looked like it had been left by a slithering snake. Some of the guys came around to help us search. We looked in the bathroom—nothing. We followed the trail to the laundry area where the clotheslines were hung. It ended there. I was praying the snake had not made its way through the small gap under my door. One of the guys lifted the lid to check inside a garbage can by the laundry area. Then he said he would look underneath the can. Ellie and I ran into my room which was right by the laundry area, and called to the "snake hunters" to let us know when it was safe to come out. The men lifted the trashcan, and there was a very large (six feet?) snake ready to strike at those who had disrupted its peaceful hideout. Quickly they brought a machete down across its neck to kill it, and somehow got it into a large black trash bag. They let us know it was safe, and as we carefully opened the door, they held up the trash bag, the snake still flopping around inside. I am thankful for the heroes who were brave enough to go after it!

One week later, the girls were again returning from Thursday evening church. One of the girls was not feeling well, so she had stayed back in her room that evening. She was in bed with the light on when the rest of the little ladies were making their way to their rooms. One of her roommates was heading for the door when she saw a green snake slither right into the room! The girls screamed and came running to get me, and the tias. One of the brave tias killed the snake quickly. After these two experiences, we spent time praying in the girls' dorm—thanking God for His protection (it could have ended very badly on both accounts) and praying that He would keep the snakes away!

Chapter 12

"I was sick and you looked after me..."

Matthew 25:36

Rita was one of the older girls living at our center. She had come when she was about twelve years old. She was very sickly, and had recently been diagnosed with diabetes. Through proper treatment, she grew healthy and strong. She would go every so often to visit her father who lived out in the bush. Alex and Ellie found out more about her father's situation, and one day we went to visit him. His house was a little house made of blocks with two small rooms. The windows were blocked up, as he could not afford windowpanes. The floors were nothing but dirt. His only piece of furniture was his bed. And that is where he spent his days. Vovo Constancio was sick. He was bedridden. He spent all of his time in a filthy little bed in a dark room. He could not get out to use the outhouse, so he used a container on the floor by his bed. His brother would come once or twice a week to give him food and refill his barrel of water that sat in the corner by his bed. The other room was dark, with a few pots and pans on the floor in the corner.

The day we visited him, we brought Rita, along with another girl and boy from the center. We put Vovo Constancio on a plastic chair and carried him outside to enjoy the beautiful fresh air. Alex and the young fellow used machetes to cut the tall grass around the house. Ellie and I cleaned the house, and the girls brought water from the well, built a fire and made lunch. After cleaning the place up, we all sat down together to eat lunch, drink tea, and chat. Vovo was so pleased to have us visit him!

It was obvious that his situation was not going to work out. Alex and Ellie and others made arrangements for him to move into one of the ministry's houses behind the children's center. A one-room addition was added onto another fellow's house, and we were so thrilled to move Vovo into his new room!

Lifting someone out of the "dust and ashes" is not just about physically making their living conditions better. Vovo was full of hurt and anger and bitterness toward his family. It may have been deserved, but most of them had abandoned him. As his condition worsened, it became increasingly harder to understand him when he spoke. Rita and others from the center would take him meals each day, and Ellie and I visited him as often as we could. We hired a couple of people to help wash his laundry, change his bedding, and bathe him. We also spent a lot of time talking to him about the Lord, praying for him, and reading to him from the Bible.

During this time, something in Rita's attitude changed. She stopped going to visit her dad. She seemed embarrassed to take him food. She started acting rude and distant and finally moved away from the center to live with relatives. We were quite confused about this shift in her character, so we prayed for her.

Some things needed to be repaired at Vovo's house, so we brought him to stay at the center for a week while the repairs were made. During that time, the lady we hired to wash his bedding and clean his house became sick and had to have time off. Alex and Ellie were visiting their family in England. I started caring for Vovo more, and the Lord used that time to teach me lessons in humility and doing the "lowest" jobs that no one would even notice. Sometimes Vovo had soiled his sheets and would feel so embarrassed as I gathered up his bedding to take out and wash. The children at the center would stop by his room to visit him. A boy named João faithfully visited Vovo every single day! He was such a delight and brought joy to Vovo. And every day I would read the Bible to him and pray with him.

We moved him back to his room behind the center. We kept visiting him, bringing him meals, getting water from the well near his house for him, sweeping his little room, and praying for him. We could no longer understand what he said. It was mostly just grunts. His hands were weak, but he could feed himself very slowly. He would always point to the end of the bed where he kept his Bible under the mattress. I would pull it out and read aloud to him from Psalms and other scriptures. Often, many of the neighbor children who knew me from the school on the center would gather in the door to listen. We saw such a beautiful change in Vovo Constancio's heart. He no longer seemed bitter and resentful about his family. He had joy!

In 2008, when my dad and sister came to visit me, they came along with me for a visit to Vovo. It meant so much to Vovo Constancio to have my dad visit him. Later Dad sent a picture for Vovo of them sitting together, and he would hold that picture in his hands—shaking his head and grinning from ear to ear with tears in his eyes.

Rita's brother returned from his wayward life and wanted to move in with his dad. One day, they called me to the house with problems. The people we hired to care for Vovo were there, and apparently Vovo's son was causing problems and inviting friends to stay in the house. I don't know what I said, but somehow it all got sorted and they were thanking me for handling the situation! I felt like I hadn't been much help at all, but it must have helped them sort things out.

Then one day, I opened my door to see who was knocking. There stood Rita. She asked if she could come in and talk to me. She told me that she realized that she had made a lot of bad choices and had done things she should not have done. She finally realized it was her own fault, and she asked God to show her what she should do now. She said He told her she needed to ask for forgiveness from Mana Anna and Mana Ellie, so she had come to ask if we would forgive her for the way she acted. After all the heartache and prayers for this dear girl, the Lord had brought her back! Of course we forgave her, and she moved in with her dad to care for him. She had changed so much and was very loving toward her dad and toward others.

After I had moved back home to Ohio, I was at work one morning and suddenly started thinking about Vovo. I felt like God said Vovo was going to die soon. That evening, I received an email from one of the missionaries to tell me that Vovo had passed away that day. Rita was sitting with him and holding his hand when he died. God had brought her back and allowed her that precious time with her dad before it was too late. I cried with sadness, but also was so glad that he was no longer suffering in his tent of a body. He was now free from his earthly struggles, and I know I will see him again in Eternity.

A couple years after her dad passed away, Rita had been dealing with an ongoing illness. She was living in her dad's house and babysat for neighbors to earn money. During one of my visits back to Mozambique, I went to see Rita. She lay in bed, weak and suffering from a continual headache. I sat on the edge of her bed, and we talked and caught up on news. She talked about how God had been so good to her. I prayed for her before leaving and gave her a hug. That was the last time I got to spend with Rita. Not long later, I received an email from a friend to break the news to me that Rita had died. I was so sad to hear this news, but again, as so many other times, so grateful how the Lord orchestrated for me to be there and have that time with her before she died. I am even more grateful how the Lord brought Rita back to Himself, and how He allowed her to have such a wonderful testimony to share with others before she died.

<u>Hospital Central</u>
(Blog journal entry – November 6, 2008)

Amina's sisters live at our center. Yesterday she came to the center feeling quite sick. The nurses in our clinic decided she should spend the night here, and in the morning we would take her to Hospital Central (our main hospital here in Maputo). Last night while we were having our missionaries' home group, the dorm mothers came looking for me and the nurses, saying Amina was having a seizure. It turned out she was sleeping in a bed and suddenly started having a seizure—eyes rolling back in her head, salivating and shaking. The nurses quickly arranged a vehicle and took her to the hospital. As they arrived at the hospital, she went into another seizure. She had no fever, so we are not sure what brought this on. She was admitted to the hospital late last night.

This morning I was at the hospital with one of the boys, for abuse counseling which we have just started taking a group of kids to. I, and one of our Mozambican educators wanted to take a change of clothes and some fruit and hygienic items to Amina. We found the ward she was in, but the guard said it was not visiting hours and we could not go in. I pleaded with them, explaining I just needed to drop off these items for her, and I would not stay to visit. Finally he allowed us to go, being careful to explain this is not normally allowed.

One of the Tias and I went up the stairs to the third floor. There was no one at the help desk, so we just walked down the hallway, which was crowded with nurses pushing carts of medicine, and doctors checking over their patient lists of the day, and we looked into each room to search for Amina. Her room didn't have any free beds left, so she was on a mattress on the floor. She had vomited in the night and still had the dirty sheets on her bed. Her stomach was still hurting, but she looked much better than yesterday. A nurse was attending her, but the doctor hadn't made his rounds to her bed yet, so we didn't get a diagnosis. We didn't wait around long, because we didn't want to get in trouble, and the doctors were busy checking the patients in that room.

As we were leaving and walking down the crowded hallway again, I saw a small room with a light on. On the floor was a mattress, with a body wrapped in a white sheet, of someone who must have just died, and they put the body there until someone could come take it away. That really shook me up seeing that.

One of the doctors I had to deal with this morning at this boy's 7:30 appointment was so disrespectful and rude to me, and the Tia. I have been praying that with going to these appointments so often (I have been 3 times in the last 4 days with 9 children!) that we would be a light of the Lord to these counselors, who are not Christians. And I felt like today I had to decide how to respond to this lady. She doesn't know Jesus. She doesn't know His love. But I believe God will open up the doors for these doctors to come to know Him. And if I am to be an ambassador, I want to represent well my Father!

It was a rough morning. I came home and spent time with the Lord. I felt very heavy and unsettled about the events that took place. I chose to forgive the doctor who spoke down to us. My devotional this morning was about being humble. Pride always goes before a fall. The Bible says over and over how the proud will be brought low, but God will raise up the lowly in Spirit.

I can be proud and shove off what people say and leave no room for God to teach me or use me. Or I can choose to humble myself, turn the other cheek, and walk on in the grace of God. It's a lesson I think I shall never finish learning until I walk into the gates of heaven.

That was my morning at the hospital.

* * *

The medical staff at our center thought we should have Amina tested for HIV, due to her continued illness. So one day,

Amina and I were dropped off at the local HIV clinic. I had been to the clinic a few times to help our nurses with some of our HIV babies and children. They had monthly check-ups here. We waited in the waiting area for a long time, in line with the countless others who came for their regular check-ups, to get their HIV medications, or to be tested. Finally, a nurse called Amina's number. We were led into a small examination room, where the nurse seated us and proceeded to explain to Amina about HIV, and what it would mean for her if she were HIV positive. She was very kind and told Amina how it would affect her life, but that it could be kept under control with proper diet and medication. She drew Amina's blood and put it on a small slide, which she set off to the side on a table. We waited for it to show up whether or not she was positive. The whole time I was really doubtful that she had HIV and was hoping it would be a negative test. Amina didn't really understand or take in what the nurse said. I think she was undereducated about this disease, so this was all brand-new information to her. Finally, the nurse asked me to go look at the slide. I walked over to the table, not completely sure by now what to expect. My eyes traveled from the nurse to Amina, and finally on the small slide that was before me. Positive. Oh! How my heart sank! I felt so overwhelmed. I could not tell Amina what the slide read; I had to wait for the doctor to tell her. The nurse passed a compassionate look in my direction, and then ushered us down the hallway to be seen by the doctor. The doctor tried to explain again to Amina about what it means to be HIV positive, and how you must control it with proper diet and medication. When it was all over, Ros came to pick us up. I shared with Ros that

Amina's test was positive. I really wanted to cry. It was all so overwhelming! I ached inside for Amina.

After returning to the center, Amina went to the girls' dorm. But soon, she was knocking on my door. She wanted to ask me some questions. I invited her in to sit and talk. "Mana Ana," she began, "what did it mean when the doctor said I am HIV positive?" So together we sat in my room, I explaining to her again what was going on in her body, how she can still enjoy her life if she receives proper treatment. She asked questions, and I did my best to answer them. Then together, we bowed our heads, and I prayed for her.

A few years later, Amina passed away. While hearing of her passing broke my heart, I also felt so grateful for the opportunity God gave to those of us who cared for her at the center. We introduced her to the saving grace of Jesus, shared with her God's unstoppable love, and got to know her sweet personality and character. She is deeply missed, but her life on this earth was not wasted just because it was cut short! She is now rejoicing in Heaven with the One who takes up our infirmities and carries our diseases.

HIV/AIDS is a disease that takes the lives of so many adults, children and babies in Mozambique each year. Many children are left orphaned when their infected parents pass away. It is a hard, cruel reality in many countries throughout the world. Several organizations are working hard to inform communities and families about HIV/AIDS, prevention, and also to provide proper medications to keep it under control and improve the quality of life for those infected with it.

CHAPTER 13

Life in Mozambique

Outreach to Manhiça
(Blog journal entry - April 26, 2008)

Last night (Friday, April 25), I joined a few fellow missionaries and Mozambicans on a one-hour trip to Manhiça—a few villages over from here. We were joining with a couple Mozambicans that work with Campus Crusade for Christ in Maputo, to show the Jesus film. This would be the first time to show the Jesus film in this village. We arrived before dark, and the guys set up the sound equipment, screen, and film projector (the old reel kind—the film was on four reels!). Ellie and I prayer walked around the area until I got called away by the Mozambican ladies to help prepare dinner. They gutted the fish and I peeled and cut up the tomatoes, onions, carrots, and peppers (and that was fine by me. I hate gutting fish!). We knelt on a reed mat and prepared the ingredients over pots. Then went to the cooking fire where we cooked a pot of beans, a pot of fish and sauce, and a pot of rice—a staple here. As we cooked it was quickly getting dark, and soon there was no light at all to see what we were doing. So the ladies would hold a stick in the fire to light the end and then hold it up over the pot so she would have enough light to check the progress.

The only noises we could hear were the bugs and tree frogs chirping away, and the little generator being revved up. The sky was incredible; layers and layers of beautiful stars! Here, without the glare of city lights, we can experience the true and natural beauty of God's creation. Millions and billions of stars layers and layers deep, flooding the sky like sparkling gems! And every so often a shooting star would fly across the sky. Seeing this reminded me how amazing our Creator God is!

That morning Pastor Andre had received the final go ahead from the village chiefs to show the film. Before then he had been told no, and he kept asking again. So the two village chiefs showed up in their little white pickup truck to see what this movie was all about. We put out 2 chairs for them, and soon a crowd had gathered—seating themselves on the ground or on grass mats as the movie began. This edition was in Shangaan, their native language.

I was still standing by the ladies and the cooking fire, and their comments went something like this: "Oh, but they didn't really speak Shangaan did they? They spoke English right?" "Look! They're baptizing them." "Oh! Look at those long beards! They must never cut their hair!" It was quite amusing.

I moved over to where the people were sitting, and they were really enjoying it. Then about twenty minutes into the film the picture cut out! The men gathered around trying to fix the machine, but couldn't manage. Pastor Andre preached a little, then Ellie's husband Alex preached. They invited people who wanted to know Jesus to raise their hand, and many did and accepted Jesus as their Savior! Then they asked who is tormented by bad dreams at night, and many more raised their hand, and we prayed for them and told them in those moments they need to call on Jesus. He is the only answer to bring them freedom from evil spirits tormenting them.

The guys handed out tracts and bible story booklets. That part was chaotic, everyone pushing and shoving and fighting to get one of those booklets. I stood guard over the projector so no one would knock it over.

Everyone was invited to come back on May 16th to watch the movie again. We blessed the chiefs each with a Bible and several of the booklets, then we prayed for them and fed them beans and rice.

The night was getting sooo cold. Many of the children who had come had sleeveless shirts on and bare legs. I can imagine they must freeze at night when they go to bed in their little grass houses, unprotected from the wind and rains.

When everyone had gone, we sat down on grass mats with the people living there, and ate beans and rice together in the dark. We said goodbyes and thank you's, and squeezed too many people in the truck, to find our way back in the dark on the sandy path ways we call "roads."

At 10:30p.m. we arrived back home, and I was showered and in my warm bed with my fleece sweatshirt on.

I love being in Mozambique! I love being out in the villages and sharing in the joys and sorrows of the people here. I love ministering to a Pastor's wife while cooking over a fire with her, and speaking a few Shangaan phrases to the old ladies sitting on the mats. I love washing dishes in little pans, drinking tea made with water boiled over a fire, going into the bushes to go to the bathroom—or in some places going into the little grass outhouse with a hole in the ground to squat over. I love seeing and hearing and smelling and breathing God's nature and feeling His love for the people here.

* * *

Visitors!

In March of 2008, I received an exciting phone call from home. My dad and sister, Cara, were coming to visit me! I prepared for weeks for their visit, planning menus and activities, setting up their rooms; dad would be sleeping in a vacant long-term missionary room, and Cara would sleep in the extra bed in my room.

The day they arrived, my missionary friend and I drove to the airport. I could hardly contain my joy as we stood on the balcony at the Maputo airport and watched the passengers exit the plane. There! We could see them as they made their way down the steps and onto the tarmac. Happy hugs and tears of joy were had, and then we had two weeks of fun—just being together! Cara got to meet for the first time all of the people she had only heard about from me. She was loved by the girls and called "Mana Anna number two." Dad got to catch up with his friends from previous visits.

We went on outreaches. We saw God multiply bread at the church on the dump. We were passing out a piece of bread to each person as they left the church. We realized that we only had a few pieces of bread left between us, but the people were still filing out. With about a dozen people still in line, we prayed silently and continued to pass out bread. As the last person left the church, we handed him the last piece of bread—and we knew that God had supplied enough for each person!

We went to Kruger National Park with a few other missionaries— getting up close and personal with two lions taking an afternoon nap right on the side of the road! We went out to eat, waded in the Indian Ocean, and most of all, just enjoyed being together. The day they left was bittersweet. I was sad to end our time together, but looking forward to seeing them again in a few months when I would be heading home for a visit.

Second Outreach to Manhiça
(During a visit from Dad and Cara - May 16, 2008)

Dad, Cara and I went to Manhiça with two missionaries and a Mozambican Pastor, as well as a few others, to show "The Jesus Film." Along the way, we picked up a fellow from YWAM who was bringing the projector for us to use. This time, the projector worked the whole time. About 300 people made their way through the village and the bush to come watch. Afterwards about 50 people came forward for the altar call, desiring to surrender their lives to the Lord. Very exciting!

During the film, Cara and I helped some ladies from the village prepare a meal for those of us involved in the outreach. We cut up carrots, peeled tomatoes using very dull knives, cut up peppers and onions, mixed it all with beans and cooked it over an open fire. We made a big pot of rice over another fire. When the people from the village returned to their homes, the rest of us sat down together in the dark to share a meal. The men sat at a dining room table that had been brought out from one of the small, one-room reed houses. The ladies sat on grass mats on the ground. One of the ladies put a towel over her arm and carried a pitcher of water and a small basin around for each person to wash their hands. The meal was served on fine china dishes —perhaps a wedding gift to one of the ladies?— that seemed out of place in this setting. The moon was full that evening, shedding a little light for us. Alex had a small crank flashlight that gave off a small bit of light as well. Everyone wore sweaters and fleeces in the chilly evening. We talked and laughed together, sharing sweet fellowship in the African bush under the stars.

A Day in the Life...
Letters Home
(October 25, 2008 – After returning from a visit home)

This morning I painted the little girls' nails and sang songs with them. I also washed all of the curtains from the girls' bedrooms and hung them out to dry. After lunch, I visited with missionary friends for a little while. Then I went back to my kitchen to make Gilda's food. Gilda has cerebral palsy and is suffering from a bedsore, so we are trying to improve her nutrition to help it heal faster. We are also trying to put some weight on her small frame. I have to use a food processor to puree her food, as she cannot chew it. Today I put in: the meat from 9 big chicken legs, 10 carrots, 2 onions, 10 cloves of garlic (garlic has a lot of healing properties), salt, pepper, turmeric, and paprika. That will be divided into portions and served with porridge. She will be getting some good meals this week! She is also getting yogurt every morning for snack, and a banana and formula for an afternoon snack. Hopefully this will help her put on weight and get healthier!

When I finished making Gilda's meals, I washed up all the dishes I had used (a ton!!). Then I got on a cleaning kick, so I scrubbed the kitchen floor, cleaned off the table that we use as a counter, cleaned the microwave, and cleaned out the toaster. It looks a lot better in there.

After cleaning the kitchen, I went to the girls' dorm for supper. The Tias said, "Aren't you sad because you have missed serving the supper on Saturdays?" And they handed me a ladle to help serve. We had rice with a cooked greens topping.

After dinner I hung all of the girls' curtains up in their rooms, and talked to some of the girls for a while. Now I am about to read my Bible and devotional and get ready for bed.

…Oh, this is something cool! I really felt while I was home that I should start a discipleship with the Tias. Yesterday afternoon, two of the Tias said, "Mana Anna, I want you to teach us. You teach the girls discipleship but you don't do discipleship with us! And we want you to start with teaching us about our relationship with God, and how to grow in our relationship with Him."

I had been holding off bringing this up to them, thinking *Oh, they would probably rather learn from a Mozambican. I don't know what they would think about me teaching them, or where to start.* I guess this was all I needed! Please pray for inspiration so I know how to do this right. It will be informal, probably more of an open discussion. Isn't God so good?!

* * *

November 15, 2008

Hi Mom and Dad!

Thanks for calling me last night. I am so happy to hear that my niece was born. Please send pictures as soon as you have them. Tell my sister and brother-in-law congratulations, and that I love them and miss them so much!

I cried for a while last night after talking to you. I really prayed because it is tough when so many exciting things are happening and I am so far from home. It was cool because I was just being honest with God, and crying and telling him how hard it is to sacrifice my family to be here. And I felt Him say very clearly to me, "Do you believe in me?" I said yes. And He said, "Do you trust in me?" I said yes. And then with my eyes shut I pictured Him reach out his big, strong, secure hand and say, "Can you take my hand?" I reached out to take it. There was something so secure about that; that I knew I could trust Him. And then peace washed over me and all the sadness left. And I was able to rejoice and be glad, and fall asleep peacefully. God is so amazing! It is still hard, but His grace covers me and I *can* take His hand and keep walking on this path He has me on.

* * *

December 13, 2008

This morning I went for a walk in the community to visit Vovo Constancio. We moved him back to his house yesterday afternoon. On the way there I bought forty four bananas to give to the girls for a snack tonight (for only $4.50!). When I arrived I discovered that he hadn't had breakfast yet. I hadn't brought anything for Vovo to eat because his son was supposed to have fed him. So I mashed up a banana for him and gave him water to drink. I read to him from his Bible, then swept the floor and brought water from the well. On the walk back to the center several little boys who attend our school were playing outside one of their houses. When they saw me coming they came running to give me hugs. They are so sweet! Then one of them asked me, "Mana Anna, out of all of us here who do you like the best?" The boys all stood, wide eyed and expectantly, awaiting my response. I don't think my response was what they wanted to hear, "I like you all the same! You are all very special and important." They really wanted to know which one of them was my favorite. They are too funny!

* * *

January 1, 2009

This morning I took Mana Sheila (she is 24 years old, and mentally handicapped) with me to go visit Vovo Constancio. On our walk home I stopped to greet this elderly lady I have come to know (well, let's say every time I pass her gate she greets me and we talk over the thorn bush "fence"). Today she is not doing well. Her legs are really bothering her. She does not speak Portuguese, only Shangaan. She just chattered on and on, but I didn't really understand anything but a few words here and there and some hand gestures. I said in Shangaan, "Can we come in and pray for you?" She said yes, so we walked through the gate, knelt down next to her on the mat, and prayed for God to heal her. After that she was filled with joy and kept saying excitedly, "Khanimambo! Khanimambo!" ("Thank you, thank you!") and then, "Hallelujah!" She said something very excitedly, but I didn't understand so I just nodded and said "Yes, yes." We left and she was still calling "Thank you!" after us. I asked Mana Sheila what she had said, and Mana Sheila began repeating to me in Shangaan what the lady had said. "Yes, Mana Sheila, but what did she say in *Portuguese*?! Translate for me!" So she did. The lady said she was so happy and when her daughter returns from her trip she is going ask if she will to take her to our church so they can worship the Lord with us.

* * *

January 10, 2009

On my way to visit Vovo today, I stopped in to see the elderly lady whose legs were bothering her. She is doing a bit better, and her daughter is back now. They want to come to church tomorrow. I hope she can make it!

And awhile back (I totally forgot about it until she brought it up!) her daughter, who must be in her late 40's, had a really bad headache and thought it was malaria. She said she always gets these headaches. I mentioned to her that our bodies need water and she should make sure she is drinking plenty of water. Today she said, "And I don't have headaches anymore! You told me to start drinking more water, and I did, and my headaches went away and I don't get them anymore!" She was so impressed. They had a neighbor lady visiting, and she was really interested to hear this and asked me, "Does it have to be cold water or just normal water?" I told her normal water is fine, either way it is fine. She was impressed to learn this, and was going to try it for herself.

* * *

Chapter 14
The Closing of a Chapter

April 2009

About a year ago, God put it on my heart to start praying for the person who would come after me in the girls' dorm. At first I thought, "I am not planning on going away any time soon!" But I did pray off and on for her; that God would be preparing the right person for the right time.

Then when I was preparing to go home for a visit last August, the Lord spoke to me that my time here was coming to an end. I went home and shared this with my parents, and prayed a lot. When I returned in October, I spoke with my leaders here, and they prayed with me, and released me to keep following God's plan for my life. We prayed for God to bring someone to fill my responsibilities here in the girls' dorm. What God called me here to accomplish in and through me has been fulfilled, and I have built on the foundation others had laid. In February, a new missionary arrived, and it was clear she was the one God had prepared for such a time as this. She truly loves the girls, and

God has blessed us with plenty of time to transition and get to become friends before I go.

I will be leaving here on April 29th and closing this amazing chapter God has written in my life. I will be sad to say goodbye to my dear friends—Mozambicans and missionaries. And it won't be easy saying goodbye to the precious daughters God temporarily placed in my care. These past three years have been a time of growth, and seeing God do so many miracles. He has protected me, comforted me, and changed me. He has shown me how big and wide and deep His love really is. He has given me compassion for those who have no hope, and taught me to hope for them, and teach them to hope. I have gotten to be a carrier of His love and life to countless babies, children and adults! It is a privilege I do not deserve—but have been given and am so grateful for.

I want to also testify that I have such peace, and God has given me such grace as He takes me from this place, to a place yet unknown. He is amazing, and I am seeing it more and more every day!

The next step…

I will be going home for a time. At first, I really struggled with just going home, and not knowing where or when I will be sent back out to the "foreign mission field." I felt God tell me to *wait*, and I feel such peace. I see that He is giving me a sweet gift of getting to spend time with my dear family for a while! I will get to see my niece who I've not met yet, and spend time with people I haven't had much time with in the last three years. I will be home at least until the end of the year (and I am so excited to be home for Christmas this year!!). In September, I plan to do a two-week medical course called "Missionary Medical Intensive," which will be very useful for a future in third world countries. And in the meantime, I am going to soak up this time with my family, share God's amazing love with those in Ohio, and *wait* on God for my next marching orders!

> *"My heart says of you, 'Seek his face!' Your face, Lord, I will seek... I am still confident of this: I will see the goodness of the Lord in the land of the living. Wait for the Lord. Be strong, take heart, and wait for the Lord." Psalm 27:8, 13 – 14*

* * *

April 28, 2009

My last evening in Mozambique:

"Dear Jesus. Bless Mana Anna because she is going. And I ask you to make her want to stay, and then we will have a big party for her. Bless the people who are in the prison. Give clothes to the people who live on the streets. Heal the people who are in the cemetery. Sleep with us in our room and protect us. Amen."

--Amelia, age 6

This is what Amelia prayed tonight as I was praying with the little girls and tucking them in bed.

* * *

I returned home at the end of April in 2009. Though I was sad to leave my girls and my dear family in Mozambique, it was also a joyful reunion to return to my family and friends in the USA!

It was not totally easy to return from living on the mission field. My family had gotten along without me, and the roles I had played three years before, were now being fulfilled by my sisters. I did not have a job for a few weeks, and it was hard to not have responsibilities. It was hard to be returning to the United States indefinitely—not just being a visitor. It was hard to see the extravagance of Americans (even the middle and lower class Americans are extravagant in comparison to most Mozambican families). I went through sort of a reverse culture shock. Though I had come home for several weeks each year for visits, I wasn't settling in and really taking a look around me. But now I was, and it was hard.

I babysat that summer for a family from church. In September, I was able to attend a two-week missionary course called Missionary Medical Intensive through Equip International. One of my missionary friends from Mozambique took the course at the same time. It was so good to catch up and talk about Mozambique with someone who had experienced the same things I had. It was also wonderful to meet many other missionaries from various countries and hear their stories. The course itself was excellent, and I learned a lot of useful information and practical skills. I would highly recommend this course if you are looking to be more useful in overseas missions.

Two weeks after the course, I joined a team of eleven from our church on a mission trip to Ukraine. My dad and my oldest brother, Greg, were part of the team, along with several close friends. It was eye opening to visit another very poor country that was not African, experience a new culture, minister to Gypsies and do children's programs in a Gypsy village. I have returned twice since then and am so blessed by the friendships that have developed with Christians in Ukraine, and the ministry opportunities we have had in that country.

Through a lot of prayer, reading a good book for missionaries returning from overseas, and also journaling my thoughts and prayers, God has really helped me to sort out the confusion and frustrations that were so prevalent when I first returned home from Africa. Over the five years that I have been living back in America, He has taught me a lot. I used to feel guilty that I was born into such a wealthy nation, and then there are the nameless babies born into the poorest of the poor families in some small village, who die from AIDS or malaria or preventable illnesses before they even reach their first birthday. Why was I privileged to be raised in a loving, Christian family—and then there is the girl who was born in "the hood" whose parents are drug addicts, whose father beats her, who spends lonely, hopeless nights in a dark room wondering what her life is all about? Why was I privileged to learn to read and write from my mother who homeschooled all ten of us, and there are adults in Africa who can't make sense of all the shapes and symbols that are actually letters and words and a whole new window of opportunity? Why were there ten healthy kids in my family, when there is Pastor Andre and his wife Maria whose babies all died before they reached two years of age?

Here is something the Lord has shown me, especially since being home the past few years. God loves the people here in

America just as much as he loves the orphans in Africa. Taking care of my elderly friends, Mr. and Mrs. Payne, as they were dying from cancer in 2010 and 2011, was just as important as taking care of babies in Africa. Ministering to girls in a Juvenile Detention Center where I have been volunteering for the past five years, and leading these hurt and broken girls to a relationship with our loving, Heavenly Father, is just as important as doing discipleship with the girls in Mozambique. God loves people. He loves us so much that while we were wicked sinners, He became a man and took the punishment for our sins—purchasing our salvation with His blood. He rose from the dead and is offering us to rise up from the sin and ashes, into new life with Him! Whether it's the thirteen-year-old Gypsy girl in Ukraine who is married and pregnant, or the thirteen-year-old girl in Africa who lives on the streets, or the thirteen-year-old girl doing her time at a detention center here in the United States, or the thirteen-year-old girl finishing up her school for the day (me!), and asking God, "What do you want to do with my life?" Each life is precious to God. He is offering each of us forgiveness, salvation and hope. Each of your lives who are reading this book, *YOU* matter to God. He is a loving Father, and you cannot earn this gift of life He is offering you. You cannot do enough "good works" to make it to Heaven. It just isn't possible. The sin gap is far too deep; the chasm is far too wide. But as the song says: "Jesus paid it all; all to Him I owe. Sin had left a crimson stain; He washed it white as snow."

The "work" that you can do is to accept the work that Jesus did and to believe in faith that what He did was enough for you – and then to begin a relationship with God who loves you and has a plan and purpose for your life!

In writing this book, my main focus and goal has been to inspire and challenge you to have a relationship with God first and foremost, and then to surrender your life to God and see where He takes you! That doesn't mean you have to be a missionary in a foreign country. He may call you to do that. But He may also call you to go to work in your office and not just pass by your coworkers, but to sit down and find out what's going on in their lives, and to tell them God loves them and sees their broken, hurting heart and wants to heal them. He may lead you to go to a nursing home to visit a bedridden elderly person who never gets visitors. To someone who needs you to sit with them, give them quality time and remind them that God sees them there in the bedroom of the facility where they reside. I don't know what God is calling you to do. But it touches His heart when you genuinely ask Him what He wants to do with your life, and then obey His leading and prompting. Following after God is not easy; it has a lot of twists and turns and unexpected experiences. But I can tell you confidently that it is worth it! That God's grace will be there for you along the way. That the sweet fellowship with God that you will experience is far greater than trying to figure out life on your own, and stumbling through, wondering if it will ever make sense.

I encourage you to ask God, "What do you want *ME* to do?" and then do it with all of your heart! He will not disappoint you.

CPSIA information can be obtained
at www.ICGtesting.com
Printed in the USA
BVOW08s2144211216
471581BV00001B/16/P